Sisters First

ALSO BY JENNA BUSH HAGER

Our Great Big Backyard
Read All About It!
Ana's Story: A Journey of Hope

Sisters First

STORIES from OUR WILD and WONDERFUL LIFE

JENNA BUSH HAGER
AND BARBARA PIERCE BUSH

Foreword by Laura Bush

GRAND CENTRAL
PUBLISHING

NEW YORK   BOSTON

Grand Central Publishing
Hachette Book Group
1290 Avenue of the Americas, New York, NY 10104
grandcentralpublishing.com
twitter.com/grandcentralpub

First Edition: October 2017

Grand Central Publishing is a division of Hachette Book Group, Inc.
The Grand Central Publishing name and logo is a trademark of Hachette Book Group, Inc.

The publisher is not responsible for websites (or their content) that are not owned by the publisher.

The Hachette Speakers Bureau provides a wide range of authors for speaking events. To find out more, go to www.hachettespeakersbureau.com or call (866) 376-6591.

From House of Lights by Mary Oliver, published by Beacon Press, Boston. Copyright © 1990 by Mary Oliver. Used herewith by permission of the Charlotte Sheedy Literary Agency, Inc.

Unless otherwise noted, photos are courtesy of the Bush family.

Print interior book design by Thomas Louie.

Library of Congress Control Number: 2017947961

ISBNs: 978-1-5387-1141-5 (hardcover), 978-1-5387-1143-9 (ebook), 978-1-5387-4543-4 (large print), 978-1-5387-2928-1 (signed edition), 978-1-5387-2929-8 (B&N signed edition), 978-1-5387-4560-1 (Target exclusive edition)

Printed in the United States of America

LSC-C

10 9 8 7 6 5

To our parents who gave us the world and to Poppy and Mila who will be sisters always.

The Summer Day

Who made the world?
Who made the swan, and the black bear?
Who made the grasshopper?
This grasshopper, I mean—
the one who has flung herself out of the grass,
the one who is eating sugar out of my hand,
who is moving her jaws back and forth instead of up and down—
who is gazing around with her enormous and complicated eyes.
Now she lifts her pale forearms and thoroughly washes her face.
Now she snaps her wings open, and floats away.
I don't know exactly what a prayer is.
I do know how to pay attention, how to fall down
into the grass, how to kneel down in the grass,
how to be idle and blessed, how to stroll through the fields,
which is what I have been doing all day.
Tell me, what else should I have done?
Doesn't everything die at last, and too soon?
Tell me, what is it you plan to do
with your one wild and precious life?

—Mary Oliver

Foreword

When I first learned I was going to be a mother, I pictured two babies in my mind. So when the doctor told George and me that we were having twins, my deepest wish was coming true. On November 25, 1981, our girls arrived, five weeks early, small and healthy, and feisty from the moment they were born. Barbara and Jenna were named for each of our mothers. Barbara arrived first, Jenna second, and from then on, George and I each had a baby to hold.

Of course, with every wish comes the famous second phrase: Be careful what you wish for. George and I had little experience with babies, and suddenly we were heading home with two. And it is not an exaggeration to say they cried all the time.

It took a few months of trial and error, but at last we adjusted to our twins and they began to adjust to the world. We knew their personalities early on. Barbara was a collector, of rocks, leaves, and piles of Easter eggs. Jenna was a homebody and a protector. When we were selling our little town house, Jenna got on her tricycle and rode in tight circles around a prospective buyer's feet, pinning her to our concrete patio.

Both girls were eager explorers, making their way into

every nook and cranny of our house, and then venturing down the sidewalk and around the block outside. Both loved to use their imaginations, creating a cat family and a language of meowing that we found adorable and their grandparents found hard to understand.

I loved every stage of their growing up, from the time as preschoolers when they scared us half to death by playing on the rocks above the ocean in Maine, to their impromptu theatrical performances, to the hundreds of times they danced up and down the hallways in our Dallas ranch house. I even loved their teenage years, although I'm not yearning to repeat them.

What I have loved most is watching them grow together. As an only child, my greatest wish was for a sister or brother. For their entire lives, Jenna and Barbara have had each other. They have been playmates, confidantes, cheerleaders, sounding boards, and dreamers. They have been partners in persuasion, right down to their relentless lobbying to get their ears pierced. Though only Jenna lobbied me to allow her to get a perm. Any night at any house could become a slumber party, and often did. When she heard ghostly noises in the White House, Jenna ran to get in bed with Barbara.

Barbara was the one who got Jenna ready for her first date with her future husband, Henry; she was the one who was there for the birth of both of Jenna's children. Jenna is the one who pushed Barbara to follow her dreams for better health for all and to start a nonprofit, Global Health Corps; she is the one who believes her sister can do anything. They can finish each other's sentences and each other's dinners. They are teaching Jenna's daughters, Mila and Poppy, the ways of sisterhood, how anything is possible if you do it together.

My daughters have kept me grounded—how could I worry about a presidential election campaign when I was worried that Barbara would wear flip-flops to Austin High School's homecoming celebration where I knew she would be crowned homecoming queen? She wore them anyway. Together, Barbara, Jenna, and I have moved in and out of houses, dorm rooms, and apartments, but never out of one another's lives.

In these pages, you will get to know the daughters, sisters, and friends that George and I know. They share some family secrets, some family bloopers, and some inside jokes. They'll tell you about being part of a big family, and a small one. They share their private memories of heartbreaking events that shaped our nation and what it's like to sit next to Vladimir Putin at dinner.

As they have grown and discovered the world, I have grown and discovered with them. We have shared travel, movies, books, and even some occasional advice on how to be a mom.

Most of all, this book is a story of sisterhood. The two girls who crammed into a tiny red toy car so they could drive side by side and for years wore matching outfits have never outgrown their special closeness. Where they once walked across the hall in a suburban house, they are now only a couple of blocks apart in one of the largest cities in the world. I am happy that my two girls have chosen to be sisters first and always. Enjoy!

—Laura Bush

Sisters First

December 23, 1994

Growing up together has been not only one of the best things in my life, but a gift from God. Many children need playmates throughout their lives to be happy. I know I have one playmate I can always count on. This particular friend doesn't live across the world, across town, or even down the street. She lives across the house. And together we've grown up loving each other. Thanks, Barbara, for always being there.

Love,
Jenna

Sisters First

JENNA

From the very beginning, before we could walk, before we could talk, Barbara and I were a pair. It wasn't just our matching pajamas and our tiny baby jeans with the same pointy green cactus stitched across each back pocket. It was that we were an unmatched set and ripe for easy comparisons: This one is the brunette and that's the blonde. She's smaller; she's bigger. She has the bright blue eyes; hers are smaller and brown. After a few years, the typecasting became a kind of shorthand: You're the loud one, right? You must be the troublemaker. Your sister's quiet. She must be an introvert.

Many of these observations were made by complete strangers. The obvious ones are accurate; my sister does have catlike turquoise eyes, while mine are beadier and brown. But were other stereotypes true or did we simply absorb them? I wonder if I become louder and more gregarious because so many people thought I was, even though I love quiet time alone. Did Barbara become more guarded and reserved because she heard others say it so often, even though she has her own strong opinions?

To much of the world, we were never really individuals; our true middle name might as well have been "and." Jenna and Barbara, Barbara and Jenna. When we walk into a restaurant or any public space together, we still invariably hear, "Oh, look, it's the Bush twins," sometimes followed by an eye roll, and then the place will fall uncomfortably quiet. *Oh, those wild Bush twins.*

But when we are apart for too long, I miss my twin terribly. Our first separation was the summer after first grade when we went to Camp Longhorn, the camp my father had loved as a boy.

Barbara and I attended different branches of the camp— "sister camps" was what they were called, ironically—across the lake from each other. For three weeks, we were apart. The initial summer, I was homesick. My first letter home was a piece of performance art, stating how many friends I had and how much I was enjoying camp. In the second, the mask came off. As only a rising second grader can, I wrote how the earlier letter had been a lie and that I had no friends *at all* and missed my family not just some but dreadfully. (Yes, I used words like "dreadfully" back then. No one has ever accused me of being subtle!)

During free time I would venture over to the cement clearing where we would have our campfires. On this ash-darkened stage, I put on a one-woman show. I didn't have an audience exactly, but in the quiet evening, my voice was within earshot. The other campers found the whole thing odd. So much so that, once, they locked me out of my cabin when I was naked. Humiliated because the boys' waterslide was nearby, I hid as best I could behind a screen door, covering my body with my chubby hands, trying to laugh it off.

The only way that I could comfort my homesick heart was to program my yellow Walkman to an AM radio station that broadcast the Texas Rangers' baseball games. Deep into the night, while everyone around me slept in their bunks, I put on my earphones and listened to the sounds of the game, the counts of balls and strikes and the solid crack of the bat connecting on a hit. I imagined my mom and my dad and my sister beside me, sitting in our usual seats. I drifted off to sleep surrounded by the people I loved.

But what I remember most from that summer is the feeling of such relief, of such pure happiness, when Barbara and I were reunited. It was a feeling of once again being made whole. For a few weeks after camp, even though we had separate rooms, we slept snuggled next to each other, lulled by the other's breathing. On those nights, Barbara's was the last voice I heard as I nodded off to sleep, and she was the first person I spoke to when my eyes opened.

We remain the finishers of each other's sentences, the conveyors of each other's dreams and desires. Again and again in all the years since, we have been the first person for each other, the one who so often knew what was in the other's heart without a word.

BARBARA

When you're born a fraternal twin, you are automatically compared, as if each twin must be the inverse of the other, a yin and a yang always slightly at odds. The shy twin versus the loud twin; the smart twin versus the funny twin; the color-inside-the-lines twin versus the creative twin. Yet I always felt that Jenna and I could simultaneously embody all these characteristics—both be smart and creative and funny, in ways that were distinct and our own.

Jenna was a hilariously creative kid who loved to perform in front of others. As second graders, she, Joanna Gikas (our best friend who lived across the street in Washington, DC), and I would create and perform endless skits, often based on movies we'd seen, for an audience of two or three: my mom and my dad and my dad's enormous 1980s video camera, which he balanced on his shoulder like a TV news cameraman on location for a live feed.

Jenna was our lead, my camera-fearing self her supporting actress. Jenna would gamely dress up in whatever costume was required—from Sebastian the crab in *The Little Mermaid* to sing "Under the Sea" to a clown for "Put on a Happy Face."

For her favorite anthem, "Castle on a Cloud" from *Les Misérables*, she carried around an old broomstick and sang every sad refrain as the lonely orphan girl. When we returned to Dallas, my mom chauffeured us around in the back of her baby blue, wood-paneled minivan so that Jenna could audition for real—*Les Miz*, *The Phantom of the Opera*, *Fiddler on the Roof*, and a host of other local theater plays. I never understood why she didn't get a callback. In my mind, Jenna was already an actress.

But in the years since, we've come to embrace that we carry within us the same traits. While Jenna's creative in a performing, audience-focused way, my creative pull finds its outlet in a quieter, introspective way. In high school and college, I studied architecture and design, and I painted for years, bold portraits, even one of Jenna. I dreamed of becoming Texas's version of Frida Kahlo.

Perhaps this inborn duality made it easier for us to navigate the public typecasting of our parents—the assumption that our dad is loud and unthoughtful and our mom quiet and bookish. Both can be true—my dad is loud and hilarious. He loves people, loves to make them laugh, and gets great joy out of putting them at ease. My mom certainly loves reading; she got her master's in library science in the 1970s. But those stereotypes capture only a tiny sliver of who they really are. My father is just as much the bookish one, a voracious reader who revels in being married to an ex-librarian. While he was in the White House, Dad and his strategist Karl Rove had an annual reading contest. The first year, Karl won, but the race was close: his 110 books read to my dad's 95. These days, Dad outreads us all.

Beneath her flats and cardigans, my mom is in fact our closet hippie and Rastafarian. When she was in her fifties and the first lady of Texas, she and I went on a mother-daughter excursion to find a Wailers show—the remnants of Bob Marley's famous reggae band—in downtown Austin. I overheard a kid in my tenth-grade art class mention that the Wailers were performing a secret concert; I excitedly told my mom the second I got home. After dinner, my mom, with her sensible hairstyle and CoverGirl lipstick, and I set out to track them down. What must the roadies have thought of a mother-daughter duo waiting in the otherwise silent music club hours before the concert while they set up speakers and tested the mics? We didn't make it to the start of the show—they were late starting and my mom had her limits on school nights—but we got close enough to read the set list taped to the stage, hinting at what we would miss.

Saturday mornings, Jenna and I would dig through Mom's record collection, playing Van Morrison, The Band, or the soundtrack from *Jesus Christ Superstar*, to which Jenna would happily perform. As a kid, I worried that my mom would leave my dad to run off with Van Morrison, because she loved his music that much.

Paul Simon's classic album *Graceland* was released when Jenna and I were in first grade, and we tagged along with my mom and her friends for our first concert. Beforehand, I spent hours picking out the most stylish item in my closet, a long red shirt emblazoned with a huge yellow pencil. Jenna and I stood on wobbly tiptoes on our concert seats when the entire crowd got up to dance as Paul sang along with Ladysmith Black Mambazo. My mom was in her element: singing, snapping her fingers, and step-touching side to side.

My mom is good at remembering names, while my dad is better at remembering people's nicknames, most of which he has given them. He has a nickname for almost everyone—and once christened, it's impossible to escape whatever he has dubbed you. Mine is "Bo-jeesh" (said, or often *yelled*, at a high volume exactly as it is spelled, an emphatic pause between the two syllables). How exactly this consonant-heavy nickname came to be, I'm unsure. I have no memory of ever entering his house or a room where he is without hearing a loud "Bo-jeesh" belted out, announcing my arrival. His loving proclamation is always met with my stifled laughter and sometimes my humiliation, especially when I was young and bringing friends home, or older and accompanied by a significant other for the first time. But these nicknames are his secret language, his way of letting us know we are uniquely special to him, an "I love you" in one-word form.

Jenna and I have one of our own. Our name for each other is "Sissy." One name, two sisters, our shorthand whether we are separated by a room or by an ocean. A word to which we both instinctively answer and turn. Because, after everything, we are sisters first.

Little Girl, Big Name

BARBARA

I was born with my grandmother's name. We both were. Knowing they were having twin girls, my parents decided the first baby to be born would be Barbara, and the second, Jenna. Alphabetical order. Neat and clean. Very my parents. I arrived first so I was named Barbara Bush. This was before Barbara Bush was first lady of the United States. Before Barbara Bush (who we call "Ganny") was truly famous. But even after she became famous, I didn't realize it. I was in the first grade. What is famous when you're six, after all? When Gampy, my grandfather, was inaugurated, I thought every family had at least one grandfather who got an inauguration, that it was a special celebration thrown for grandfathers. One big party and America shows up because America loves grandfathers. I remembered all the talk of "our forefathers," so I had just conflated the two.

I was so immersed in my particular self-generated lore that

I started wondering when my friends' grandfathers' inaugurations would be. Would their parades also be bitterly cold and full of loud horns and marching bands and brightly colored uniforms? When Ganny came to visit Preston Hollow Elementary School to show off our new puppy Spot, daughter of her famous dog Millie, I was far more impressed to see the sixth graders who came out of their classrooms to line the hallways than I was by the concept of a first lady's visit.

My parents' single-minded determination to de-emphasize that there was anything unduly special about being a Bush meant that I didn't understand why my name might make me different. I already lived in a sea of Georges, where multiple generations would easily turn around the moment the word was uttered. My father had his father's name, and my older cousin, George P. Bush, was also, obviously enough, a George. (In recent years across Africa, I have even met a cohort of young "George Bushes," including George Bush Mudariki, kids who are alive due to the medications delivered by PEPFAR, the AIDS relief program my dad started, and who were named in his honor. There are many ways to be a namesake.) For my part, I was simply holding up the female line, which was why I had my Ganny's exact same name: Barbara Pierce Bush.

But when you have the same name as the first lady of the United States, there are times when "the name talk" would have been helpful. As an eight-year-old, I would offer to order pizza for our family, relishing my mature and responsible position.

"I'd like to order a pizza."

"Great, your name?"

"Barbara Bush."

"This isn't funny."

Aggressive click.

What…? I was constantly hung up on, whether I was ordering pizza from Domino's, school supplies from a catalog, Girl Scout cookies, or books from the shiny Scholastic flyers we brought home from school. No one believed that First Lady Barbara Bush wanted to order *Miss Nelson Is Missing.* Little girl, big name.

After each such episode, I felt ashamed—ashamed of some behavior I didn't understand. I was clearly in trouble, but I had no idea what I had done wrong. So I told no one. Instead, I would meekly go off to get someone else to place my order, further cementing the myth of my own shyness. It never occurred to me to simply give a different name.

Then came high school. At Austin High, the first moment of the first day of school started with homeroom. I'd walk in, nervously wondering who I'd see. Inevitably, roll would be called, and, the "Bs" came quickly. "Barbara Bush?" Quietly: "Here." Boys in the back would then snicker loudly, "Oh, snap! Barbara Bush!" Snap, indeed.

The irony was that I didn't really know the iconic Barbara Bush back then. Outside of the year we lived in DC when we were in kindergarten, whenever we saw Ganny, it was with a crowd of other relatives. I was one of ten or twenty, somewhere in the middle of the long line of cousins from five families. One summer, as a little girl, I even learned needlepoint so that Ganny and I might have something uniquely in common, something that we could do together. Neither Jenna nor I spent any real individual time with her until we turned sixteen; we were adults before we got to know the nuances of her personality, to see her as more than the white-haired woman in pearls who shooed us out to play and made us hang up our wet towels when we tramped back home.

And, perhaps, as she grew older, she became more accessible and playful as well. Sixty-year-old Barbara Bush might not have worn two different-colored sneakers, but by age eighty, she loved to pair a pink shoe with a red one from her closetful of colorful Keds.

Today, babies who were born when my grandfather became president are themselves close to turning thirty, but the passage of time has not necessarily made it any easier to be Barbara Bush. Not too long ago, I showed up to give a speech on global health, and many of the attendees expected my grandmother to walk out onstage, not her thirty-something-year-old granddaughter, Barbara Bush 2.0.

Even now, when I show my ID at security to enter a building in New York City, I'm almost always met with a reaction. The guard will look at it, look up at me and smile, and 3, 2, 1... "I'll bet that name's caused you a lot of trouble." You can say that fifty more times.

And of course, there is the minefield of interfamily communication, like the time when my cousin Wendy sent an e-mail to me, cousin Barbara Bush, asking for advice about bikini waxing and electrolysis, starting with the classic line, "Yo, how are ya?" But when she typed the name into the box, Ganny's address populated. Unknowingly, Wendy hit Send. Ganny didn't bat an eye. She wrote back, advising Wendy to stay far away from harsh products like Nair, and closed the e-mail by saying she was looking forward to seeing her in Maine. Wendy was (and still is) mortified.

For years, I dealt with the famous strings attached to my name per my formidable grandmother. It was when my father became president that it got tricky yet again. I coined some new last names for myself for specific instances. Dinner reservations were under Barbara McBabson. Or Barbara Catswith (because I love cats). Introductions to new people were met with ad hoc aliases to fend off the inevitable deluge of questions. I wasn't always so eloquent in the moment… "I'm Barbara. Uh, Barbara Barbara."

According to current baby dictionaries, the name Barbara is going the way of the dinosaur, on a sharp decline toward extinction (except for Eastern Europe—go, Eastern Europe!). Barbaras under the age of forty are a rare breed, overshadowed by the Barbara powerhouses of older generations: Barbra Streisand, Barbara Walters, and, of course, Barbara Bush.

When you're one of the last remaining Barbaras, you have a role to play, bearing the name proudly and unabashedly— and I hold my head up slightly higher because "we" are at the end of the line. Except that in many ways, I'm not much like those famous Barbaras. In temperament, I'm far more like Jenna Welch, my other grandmother, the gentler, self-taught naturalist of Midland, Texas, than I am like my fiercely outspoken Ganny. It is Jenna Bush Hager who most closely resembles the original Barbara Pierce Bush.

But I do love my name. As a girl, I was told it meant "beautiful stranger." I'll take it. In that regard, my parents made a good choice: I do appreciate the beauty in others, and every close friend of mine, from all over the world, began as a stranger, just as I began as a stranger to them—even if at the beginning, they recognized my name.

Accidentally Famous

JENNA

Our lives were not dysfunctional, but they were at times strange. We were photographed from the moment we were born, not cute family snapshots, but photos taken by real photographers with camera bags and telephoto lenses. Less than an hour after we were born by Cesarean section, my mother, swollen with edema from her failing kidneys and preeclampsia, was being wheeled back from the operating room and a photographer jumped out from behind a wall in the Baylor Hospital maternity ward. He started taking pictures of her exhausted, bloated face, and she was so stunned that she tried to smile. Fortunately, it was the photo of my smiling father, balancing two swaddled bundles in his arms, that flashed across the country on the wire services with a headline about Vice President Bush's new twin grandbabies. We were "accidentally famous" from the moment we were born.

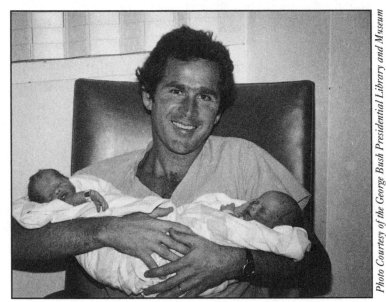

Photo Courtesy of the George Bush Presidential Library and Museum

Our first baby photo, which went out on the wire services, with the caption, "The Vice-President's newest twin granddaughters."

When our dad's parents came to visit us in Midland, Texas, it was not for Father's Day or Thanksgiving, but for public events like campaign rallies. In 1984, when we were not yet three, we were given "grown-up" seats on a stage and decked out in matching blue polka-dot dresses with white collars and white pinafores. Barbara sat in her seat, but I ended up down on the stage floor, scooting around under my grandmother's watchful eye. At one point, I lifted up my dress right as my grandfather was speaking, and the cameras went wild. I don't remember any of it, but I know it happened—the afternoon superimposed into my childhood memory album—because photographers captured it all.

We wore our fancy clothes to events like the White House

Easter Egg Roll, where we stood with our grandparents and a massive rabbit in a gingham dress on the perfectly clipped green White House South Lawn. When we had playtime with our cousins, it was captured by TV cameras for live television as we ran around on a brightly lit stage after a balloon drop at a Republican National Convention.

But there were also times when being famous, even accidentally, hurt. I first heard the word "wimp" on the playground during recess when I was a kindergartner at an elementary school in Washington, DC. I knew from the sound of it that I did not want to be a wimp at any cost. When a sixth grader said to me, "I bet you can't do an apple flip off the monkey bars," I climbed right to the top. I didn't know what an apple flip was; the only gymnastics move I could do was a somersault, on the ground. But I wanted to be the courageous girl who could stand on the top of the monkey bars and dive off, so I did. I don't recall anything about my brief moments of flight, only that I crashed to the hard ground beneath and broke my jaw. Barbara says that all she remembers was seeing my teal-and-white-striped T-shirt with a bloody handprint on the front.

I didn't realize that the word "wimp" existed beyond the school playground until I stood in the supermarket checkout line with my mother in Washington, DC. I saw a *Newsweek* magazine with Gampy on the front cover and the word "wimp" next to his face. I was confused. My grandfather, who babysat us, who kept in continual touch with his children and grandchildren, first through letters and later via e-mail, who had fought in World War II, was anything but a wimp. Staring at that cover, I felt embarrassed. I wanted to turn over the magazine, to look away. Because on some level I realized that if my mom and I could see it in the supermarket checkout line, so could everyone else. I asked my mom why Gampy's photo was next to the word "wimp," and she gave me whatever reassuring answer she could. The next time I saw Gampy, I was ashamed to associate him with the magazine. Even if the public figures in my family—Gampy and Ganny, and later my dad and my mom—were going to appear on the pages of magazines, as an elementary schooler it never occurred to me that I would be anything but anonymous. Sometimes I managed to remain out of the public spotlight in spite of myself.

When I was seven and staying at my grandparents' house in Maine, my older cousins convinced me that maxi-pads were used for underarm sweat. After I stuck them to my armpits, those same cousins dared me to walk downstairs to say hi to all the grown-ups gathered in the living room. But it was not just the usual family and close friends. Deng Xiaoping, the paramount leader of China, was visiting Gampy, along with his aides and an unusually large contingent of international photographers, ready to snap away. Luckily for me, as I made my grand entrance, the cameramen must have realized there are some photos that are just too awful to take.

By the time my dad was in the White House, my luck with anonymity was gone. In retrospect, where it hurt the most was in the classroom, my classroom. At the start of 2005, after my dad won reelection, I began working as a teacher at the Elsie Whitlow Stokes Charter School in Washington, DC. At school, I was "Miss Jenna," no last name. I began my day in the multipurpose room where teachers graded papers and the kids ate breakfast, rewarmed pancakes or cereal. The staff put out newspapers around the room to encourage the kids to read.

I had a student, Yvonne, who was smart and observant. On a Monday morning after the inauguration, she came up to me with one of those newspapers and pointed to a photo of Henry Hager, now my husband, and me dancing at one of the balls. The angle of the photo made it look like an over-the-top, sexy dance, and although I was holding a Diet Coke in my hand, in the photo it looked like it was an alcoholic beverage. Yvonne said, "What are you doing in this picture?" as if she were asking me for confirmation.

Up until a minute before, I had been standing in a room that smelled vaguely of syrup, thinking about my lesson plan and ways to get to know the kids and for them to get to know me. Then my cover was blown.

I understood Yvonne's curiosity, though. When I was her age, I had a deep fascination with the printed page, particularly with magazines, and for years, I, too, believed the stories told by the glossy pictures and the beguiling words. It was only as a young adult that I came to really understand what it can be like for those standing on the other side.

Before there was the term "fake news," there was, well, fake news—snippets of outrageous stories that made the press or ended up on the Internet. I read stories in the tabloids that I was dating men I had never met; some people sold the made-up stories for money. My Wikipedia page was changed every month to report that I was pregnant when I wasn't—my mom blamed my love of bohemian tops. I saw press reports that Barbara and I had run naked through a hotel in Mendoza, Argentina, when we have never set foot in the city. When I flashed the symbol of "hook 'em horns" for University of Texas during my dad's inauguration, a Danish paper showed the photo and reported that I was a devil worshipper. I've learned to never google myself.

At this point of my life, though, I have become fair game for all kinds of tabloid fodder. Indeed, you could argue that everything that happens to me in print, online, and on film is entirely my doing, because I'm the one who chose a job in television.

Home Port

BARBARA

Growing up, we were at times a nomadic family, packing up boxes and pulling up stakes every few years. We left Midland, Texas, in 1987 for eighteen months in Washington, DC; then to Dallas; then off to Austin; then back to Washington. The longest we lived in one city was in a public building, the grand, white-porticoed Texas governor's mansion, our family tucked away in an upstairs "apartment" surrounded by "official rooms." Many afternoons, we were reschooled on the basics of Texas history, eavesdropping as tour guides and tourists wandered the floor below.

Though I'm proudly Texan (that's how we do, y'all), I haven't lived there in years. My apartment in New York is purposely spare, with few possessions. As a professional wanderer, I've never wanted to accumulate many things. I take great pride in being a minimalist—never checking luggage, no matter how long the trip. The only constant place in my life for thirty-five years has been the tip of a point, Walker's Point, in southeastern Maine.

Every summer, my sister and I would count down the days until we'd head to Maine. Our huge family—thirteen cousins in the early 1990s plus our aunts and uncles—would decamp to Kennebunkport for weeks at a time. The Point was always centered around our grandparents, especially our gentle grandfather. He'd use the sea and family to relax away from the politics in Washington, DC. In an era before e-mail or cell phones, we had almost no contact with our cousins during the school year, but that only made the anticipation of seeing them again the next summer all the more thrilling. What would their lives be like now? Their interests? Would George P. still be into *The Karate Kid*? Would Wendy and Noelle, who were five years older than us, still be slightly out of reach?

Our days were spent entirely outside, chasing our cousins in the yard; playing hide-and-seek in the fragrant, prickly raspberry bushes; or down by the water, playing pirate on the jagged ocean rocks, jumping off the dock into the bitterly cold Maine bay, competing for who could stay in longest. We'd linger well past sunset, whiling our days away until our parents called us in for dinner or bed—each of us reluctantly emerging from Ganny's garden, or the rocky beach, a perfectly tired crew of freckled, pink-skin-splotched, grass-stained cousins. Lunches were picnics, turkey sandwiches eaten on beach towels, the bread and meat crunchy with salt and sand.

At night, we'd sit at the "kids' table." My uncle Jeb's oldest son, the mature and well-behaved George P., was the only cousin allowed to join the "grown-up table," sitting among the group that included the prime minister of Canada or other foreign dignitaries discussing foreign affairs; or Hollywood producers, who in later years we'd find interesting, but at the time bore no relevance to our next day's adventure.

We were our own entertainment directors. One rainy summer, we watched the movie *Grease* seventeen times, memorizing all of the lyrics and performing them in a cousins-only chorus. We wrote and performed skits for an audience of our aunts and uncles, and in bad weather we camped out in the dark wooden closets in the attic, whispering as we hid from adults and breathed in the slightly musty cedar scent. We learned the legend of Bloody Mary—how reciting her name three times while gazing in a mirror was supposed to reveal her standing behind you. Before bed, we'd dare each other to call forth her spirit. Chills running down my spine—"Go look, Barbara; go look"—I would summon the courage to gaze into the ancient, tiny attic mirror and dutifully repeat her name. For hours after, I'd lie awake, too scared to doze off. To this day I still get chills climbing up to the attic, in case Mary is waiting.

Ganny made the rules, which hung on the back of each bedroom door: children outside in the fresh air in the daytime and summer reading before bed at night. We slept in what we called the "Girls' Dormitory" (with George P. the token guy)—the attic outfitted with a line of twin beds and, in a throwback to another era, bright teal carpeting and matching walls. Being allowed to sleep in the dormitory was a rite of passage—when Jenna and I were young, a night there was a special treat. We would head up with our pillows and nightgowns, too young to wear cool pajamas, and stay up for hours. Once we were old enough to have a permanent bed, we would snuggle under our tightly tucked sheets and read *Little Women* or *The Borrowers* until someone turned off the lights and one by one we dropped off to sleep listening to the sound of the ocean.

In the mornings, we would bound from our beds and race to our grandparents' room. There, in a mass of oversized T-shirts and summer pajamas, all jumbled limbs and sleep-matted hair, we would climb into their bed and snuggle up next to Gampy as he read the paper. Our parents and aunts and uncles would make their own way in, coffee in hand, three generations in one space under one roof.

Almost always, though, the highlight of the summer was when Gampy would take us out with him on the water. His boat was named *Fidelity*, and it was built for speed. He enjoyed nothing so much as slicing the sleek bow through the ocean swells, pushing the throttle forward when we hit big waves to make us bounce and laugh and yelp with pleasure. But he did not race past beauty, like the tiny uninhabited islands where seals gathered to sun their gleaming wet bellies and backs and porpoises swam in tight schools. Sometimes he would stop to fish, but even more fun than casting the baited hooks and pulling in the blues was having the companionable silence and full attention of our sweet grandfather.

Once when I was in my early twenties and Gampy in his early eighties, we got stuck out on the boat in a beautiful heavy rainstorm. There was no fear with Gamps as the driver: He was a superb skipper. He sped at sixty miles per hour through the huge, wind-whipped swells, with lightning bursting around us, and fish arcing up in the waves alongside—a parade guiding us home. And as I looked at him, rain pelting his face, he threw his head back and howled with joy at the magnificent ocean and his wild crew of family members urging him on. In the distance, a rainbow appeared.

———————

On October 12, 2003, Gampy sent this e-mail to his grandkids:

Subject: Leaving and crying.

In exactly 69 minutes we drive out the gate of the Point we love so much.

The trek back to Houston begins. We speak at West Virginia Monday, then fly back to Houston Monday evening.

Yesterday Bill Busch and I took a final run in Fidelity. It was heaven. Swells but no real chop on the sea. There were tons of mackerel breaking the water but no blues, no stripers chasing them. We did see some tuna, obviously in quest of a mackerel lunch. I left Bill off on his boat here at the point then roared back to the river going full blast. I am sure it was over 60. I felt about 19 years old.

The only thing wrong with the last five months is that none of you were here enough. Oh I know some got to stay as long as usual, but there never can be enough of having all of you here. Next year, promise this old gampster that you will spend more time with us here by the sea.

I am a very happy Gampy. My legs don't bend too well. As you know I have had to give up fly fishing off the rocks, but there is plenty left to do—plenty of wonderful things. I think of all of you an awful lot. I just wonder how each of you is doing—in life, in college, in school.

If you need me, I am here for you, because I love you very much. This comes from your devoted,

Gampy.

PS—I never went in the ocean this year. The first time in my 78 years here (I missed 1944) that I haven't gone in. Sad am I, but I got huge kicks of seeing you dive off the pier. I got a clear shot at that from Jean's office window. Sadie just came in. She is very nervous. She sees the bags. She knows Ariel, Paula and Alicia left a week ago. Now she prances around viewing the horrid suitcases wondering what's next for her. She'll be OK in Houston but she'll miss Kport—of that I am sure.

Photo Courtesy of the George Bush Presidential Library and Museum

---

Operation Spikey

BARBARA

I don't remember my grandfather running for president. What I do remember is the one time when we were in kindergarten and he took Jenna and me and our cousins to the circus. During the performance, he stood on the dirt floor in the center of the tent and threw a tall top hat into the ring, literally acting out the phrase "throwing your hat in the ring." (For trivia fans, that's how Woodrow Wilson announced his run for the presidency at the Ringling Brothers, Barnum and Bailey Circus. For years, other candidates continued the tradition.) I didn't realize the magnitude of the moment—he was just Gampy, onstage with the all-powerful ringmaster. I was mesmerized by the lights, the acrobats, the clowns, and, most important to me at the time, the big cats: the lions and tigers performing for the crowd. Slow, deliberate, and fierce. As a souvenir, we each got a stuffed animal. I chose a white tiger I named "Spikey" that became my constant companion.

I slept with Spikey, played with Spikey; I brought him every-where, including to my grandparents' house in DC when they would babysit and Jenna and I would spend the night.

We loved spending the night with Gampy and Ganny. They lived in an old white house with slick wood floors and a great, wide staircase, perched on the top of a hill. Below, on all sides, was an enormous, grassy yard with a slope that was per-fect for rolling down. It was the vice president's house, but to us, it was just a huge home, perfect for fun. Jenna and I would spend the day playing make-believe in the house and running through the grounds. And it was somewhere out there one night, catching fireflies that fluttered their wings and blinked out their flashes of code, tramping through the magnificent dusk, that I was sure I had lost Spikey. Ganny and Gampy were about to tuck us in when I realized I didn't have my stuffed friend. I was devastated, my legs dangled off the side of the bed as I sobbed. I couldn't possibly lie down without him. Gampy, who is quite a good crier himself, couldn't bear it. He grabbed a flashlight and went in search of Spikey. Of course, when the vice president goes searching in the dark for a stuffed tiger, he doesn't go alone. A small phalanx of Se-cret Service agents followed him, flashlights in hand, on the Spikey search-and-rescue mission.

But when you are six years old and exhausted, you can cry for only so long before you collapse on your covers and fall asleep. That's exactly where Gampy found me when he came back hours later, empty-handed. "Operation Spikey" would have won Gampy some amazing grandfather points on any or-dinary night, but this one was far from ordinary; it was the night before a presidential debate. Most candidates would be cloistered away, briefing books in hand, rehearsing possible answers as some well-spoken senator played the opponent and aides played the moderators. But for George H. W. Bush, it wasn't even a decision. Spikey had to be found.

And we did find him, the next morning, when we pulled back the curtains to let in the sunshine. He was camped out under the window. Jenna and I had been playing house behind the curtains, and Spikey had spent the night tucked beneath them. Gampy won that race; and sixteen years later, I would carry a tattered and largely de-stuffed Spikey in my suitcase for my dad's last campaign, a good-luck talisman.

I didn't understand the gravity of my grandfather being president, probably because he didn't speak about it. While he never hid the fact that he was president, Gampy didn't want us to think of him that way. He didn't want us to be impressed by titles. Rather, he wanted to teach us that it was the family moments, the light moments, and the joyous moments, on which we should make our lasting memories. When it came time to record his own memories of us at our father's inauguration, he didn't make sweeping pronouncements about the gravity of the moment. What he noticed—and even fretted over—were the small personal details—the thought of us watching the protesters and especially what he termed our "craziest" high heels:

> Jenna and Barbara looking lovely in their new dresses were to be announced just before us. The twins had on the craziest high heels I have ever seen. In the holding room both had kicked off their shoes to alleviate the pain caused by walking on the stilt like heels—thin, tall, pointed heels, like spikes. Anyway off we all went the girls wobbling on their stilt-heels, Bar and I grin-

ning like Cheshire Cats and waving to a lot of Capitol Staff and Capitol Police who lined the wall waiting for Presidents #42 and #43 to appear.

The twins preceded us, each on the arm of a 3 stripe military officer. Gone was their cocky banter from the holding room, their feigned nonchalance and indifference left behind.

One sad thing though, Jenna and Barbara, riding with us, seemed very concerned about the demonstrators. I tried to assure them not to worry because this simply went with the territory, all Presidents suffer through this kind of ugliness; but they were not convinced. They hated the signs and the shouting and the vulgarity of it all. I worry about the effect of this kind of thing on these two vulnerable 19 year olds.

Losing Pa

JENNA

There are buildings, libraries, schools, highways, even an airport, the George Bush Intercontinental Airport in Houston, named after one of my grandfathers. He has been the subject of books, articles, and documentaries. But Barbara and I had another grandfather, our precious Pa.

Pa had so many hopes for us, but I can't imagine that chief among them was that we would become the keepers of his memories so soon. After we turned twelve, he stopped knowing who we were, and we were left with only a shell of him. I can look through old photos and see how in the span of a couple of years, his twinkling eyes suddenly became flat and vacant. More than twenty years after his death, I still wish that our last memories of him were as gentle as our first ones. If I could rewrite his story, I would give Harold Welch, our Pa, an easier ending.

Pa was born in Lubbock, Texas, the younger of two sons. He met Jenna Hawkins, the Jenna for whom I am named, when they were both living and working in El Paso. It was a quick, wartime romance; Harold Welch had enlisted in the Army at age thirty. They were married in January 1944, just as he was about to be shipped off to Europe with his unit, the 104th Infantry, known as the Timberwolves. After he returned in 1946, they moved to Midland, Texas, and for the rest of Pa's life, Midland was home.

Laura Welch, our mom, was Harold and Jenna's only surviving child. Barbara and I were their only grandchildren, and Pa and Grammee were a presence in our lives from the moment we were born. There was something about him that seemed big, and not simply because we were small. His not-quite-six-foot height was made larger by the fedora that he always wore to cover his bald head, and he had a bigger-than-life presence about him.

By the time we knew him, Pa wore big black orthopedic shoes that clunked and squeaked whenever he took a step. He was also a perpetual whistler, not just a few bars, but verses of entire songs. The mockingbird that nested in his backyard emulated his version of Elvis's "Please Release Me." Long before we laid eyes on him, we would hear him coming, walking and whistling.

When we were babies, every afternoon he would walk up to the door of our house and call out in his booming voice, "Laura, are the girls up?" knowing full well that even if we weren't, we would be now. From deep inside our cribs, he lifted us to hug him and we nestled ourselves against his chest, breathing in the scents of the coffee and cigarette tobacco, which clung to his shirts even after they were washed and dried in the blazing West Texas sun. He drank coffee all day, a cup with Grammee in the morning, then another with his buddies, and still more at his various stops across Midland.

The only day he didn't come by our house at naptime was on Saturdays during football season. On those Saturdays, he would drive from the ranch-style brick house that he had built on Humble Avenue (after Humble Oil; many of Midland's streets were named for oil companies) over to Johnny's Barbecue, a West Texas institution owned by his best friend, Johnny Hackney. Both Johnny and Pa had piercing blue eyes and shiny bald heads; they could have been brothers. Johnny's Barbecue was impossible to miss; even as small children we could spot the redbrick building adorned with a giant pig sign in the heart of downtown Midland. Inside was a smoke pit. Johnny didn't believe in fancy seating; diners chose from a line of worn wooden picnic tables. We ate there many times, our faces sticky with smoke rub and barbecue sauce. As often as we visited Johnny's, we never ventured into his mysterious back-room office. But that was where Pa went every Saturday.

Inside, about half a dozen men, dressed in creased pants and crisp white shirts that their wives had ironed on washday, would sit around a folding card table, their eyes glued to the small TV in the corner of the room. Hour after hour, they lit unfiltered Marlboro Reds, drank Johnnie Walker out of Styrofoam cups, and bet their hard-earned dollars on college football—or so our mother said.

Our grandfather, like many men in West Texas, was a gambler. The boom-bust economy of oil and cattle, gushers and droughts, made cards, dice, horses, and football betting seem like ordinary risks. At various times, Pa bet on everything, especially horses and dice—my mother remembers coming home with a college boyfriend to the sight of her father and his friends shooting craps on Grammee's freshly scrubbed kitchen floor, the dice skidding across the tile and bouncing off the yellow cabinets—but probably his biggest bet was on life itself. Having lived through the deprivation of the Depression, he had enough faith and gumption to leave the security of his traveling sales job and strike out on his own, building homes for the newcomers who were flooding into West Texas during the postwar oil boom. Yet, while he loved some risk, there was nothing restless or calculating or mean about Pa. Neither Barbara nor I can ever remember seeing him truly mad.

When we were small and I was clumsy, dropping food from my fork or spilling my glass of milk all over the kitchen floor, he would say "Happy Days," even before my grandmother could reach for her rag to start wiping or Mom's face would tense in frustration. His response to everything was "Happy Days" and a smile. He never yelled. I know now that Pa and Grammee always wanted a houseful of their own kids. Pa and Grammee adored children. They adored us, and we were the answer to their prayers.

As a child, I was a boundary pusher, the one who would touch the hot stove, just to see. Sometimes I tried to get my sweet Pa to lose his temper. The focus of my efforts on one particular afternoon was an innocuous Kleenex box that he kept in the front console of his old Buick. Car seats and booster seats were unknown in a place where money changed hands over Texas Tech and Arkansas Razorback games; when Pa and I drove around Midland's dusty streets, I rode shotgun. During the drive, I manually rolled down the old-style passenger window, grabbed the tissue box, and hurled it out of the car. Without a word, Pa put on his blinker and applied the brake. He pulled over to the shoulder and slowly got out of the car. There was a stiffness to him as he bent to retrieve the Kleenex from amid the trash and tumbleweeds. After he had walked back, seated himself, and repositioned the box, he calmly asked me—without a trace of anger—not to do it again. His old voice was full of patience and love. He pulled back onto the road, and a few minutes later, I grabbed the box and tossed it out again. I did it several more times, and each time, his reaction was the same.

I'm not sure why he never put the tissue box out of my reach or told me not to roll down my window or simply put me in the backseat; perhaps he was trying to teach me the difference between quick impulse and quiet strength. Again and again, I tested this man, whose patience never broke.

Our Midland lives were rich in simple moments. When Pa took walks around the block, we would scamper along with him. When Pa sat on the porch to watch the world go by, along with the occasional car, we watched with him. By the time we were six, Midland had ceased to be our day-to-day home; our parents moved us to Washington, DC, so that my dad could work on Gampy's presidential campaign. Away from Midland, Pa and Grammee were no longer part of our daily lives. They were now special visitors, our memories crammed into a yearly Thanksgiving meal or a rare family trip to Disney World, where after each ride we scanned the crowd for the comforting sight of the top of Pa's fedora. Or each summer, when, for a week or so, we went "home" to Midland.

Our first-ever solo commercial flight was from Dallas to Midland when we were seven. Barbara and I were eager to board the plane, just the two of us, and arrive to see Pa and

Grammee as close to the plane door as they could get, faces beaming. From the beginning of the trip, clutching our small suitcases, we felt emboldened and older than we were. (Why do kids always want to grow up so fast?) We also couldn't wait because in Midland, Pa and Grammee spent their entire day with us, except when they took their naps in the afternoons. When the heat was so fierce in the summer that even the asphalt seemed to liquefy, the only reasonable thing to do was sleep. Unless you were a kid determined to prove that you were long past napping.

We passed that time digging through Grammee's sewing room, which doubled as our bedroom, and her collection of spare buttons, ribbons, and fabric scraps. When we grew tired of that, we turned our attention to what we dubbed the memory cabinet. The memory cabinet was a large Victorian bureau that had been Pa's mother's. Inside its doors was a well-organized archaeological dig into our family's younger lives. There were shelves with photo albums, yearbooks, shoe boxes full of postcards, and handwritten letters tied in packets with string. We flipped through pages, looking at photos of our mom in her puffy 1950s embroidered skirts and cat-eye glasses. Until we found one box filled with memories that Pa would have preferred we never find.

It was Barbara who opened that box and began picking out photos, staring at them slowly, one by one, and asking, "What are these?" I looked. They were tiny black-and-white photos, but their smallness did nothing to diminish what we saw: mountains of bodies arranged in long rows; all naked, ribs protruding, limbs contorted. We dropped them back into the box, afraid to touch them. "Did Pa take these?" I asked Barbara. "Why would he have them?"

"Pa, what are these?" was our first question when we heard the sound of his footsteps in the hall.

He didn't want to tell us the history of what he had seen as an American soldier helping to liberate Nordhausen, a Nazi death camp, at the end of World War II. The man who smiled and found "Happy Days" in small calamities did not want to talk to us about those days or that time. We hadn't even known that he fought in the war. He left the details of the explanation to Grammee. He never hid his photos from us; they were there each time we looked. It was as if he had taken in the images of those suffering people and given them shelter in a solid wood cabinet deep inside the safe world of Midland.

It seemed far away down the hall, but in reality our bedroom and Grammee and Pa's room were so close that as we fell asleep, we could hear the murmurs of their conversation, soft whispers, and then the sound of Pa's snores, punctuated by the occasional passing car, until we drifted off toward the morning. In the same way, I thought that the steady rhythm of our summers would continue indefinitely. Then our precious Pa began to change.

It was small things at first: calling us by each other's names, forgetting the name of the restaurant we had dined in for lunch, or not recalling the funny winning phrase from a *Wheel of Fortune* episode that we had watched together the night before. Then came the summer when we were twelve, the summer when our Pa was no longer Pa. This year, there would be no rides in the Buick, no trips to Johnny's Barbecue, no lazy strolls around the block.

We were there when Pa bolted out the front door and took

off down the street, moving as if he were on a mission—but without any destination in mind. Grammee raced after him, her short legs rushing to keep up with his long strides. We followed her until we caught up with Pa. Even then, he wouldn't slow down, wouldn't listen to our pleading. Barbara and I looked at each other, confused and scared. We didn't understand what was happening; it was as if someone had taken over our grandfather. Eventually, he grew exhausted and sat down on the curb. His breathing was rapid, his eyes vacant. Nothing could budge him. We tried to help Grammee lift him up to get him back home, but we couldn't; our arms were too weak and he was too stubborn. Grammee rushed back to the house to call the fire department, while we waited, helpless, sitting beside him on the curb. Just as he had shown me such patience on our now long-ago car ride, it was our turn to be patient.

It was the last walk we ever took.

Even worse was the shame that settled over Pa. For a man who never punished us—who never inflicted shame—in that last year, he was overcome with it. He had moments when his brain believed that he had lost all his money to gambling. Thinking he was broke, he would beg my father for a loan. My dad would say, "Of course, Harold. We can do that," trying to reassure Pa. He had fleeting moments of lucidity when he knew or seemed to know that he was in the grip of a disease. Lying in the twin beds of our room, Barbara and I heard him wake at night: We would hear Grammee's gentle snores, and then the moment when the mattress would creak and the bed frame shudder and Pa would sit bolt upright. We held our breath and listened. He sobbed over what he had said or done. We heard Grammee try to console him, but he was inconsolable. The next morning, no one said a word. But we had heard everything.

Then there was the one lunchtime in the yellow kitchen with its Formica counter, where nothing had changed since our mother was a girl. It was the same kitchen where on countless nights we had sat on our favorite stools and watched Grammee make her meat patties, little sirloins that she pounded down and cooked in a skillet until they tasted better than anything. It was the warm and familiar place where Barbara and I had made so many of our memories.

I was twelve, in the sixth grade. The previous fall, we had transferred from a public school to an all-girls private school in Dallas. Walking down the school's wide hallways was like visiting a foreign country; everything was bigger and shinier than in our old elementary school. The girls seemed smarter and fancier, brasher and bolder, prettier, and sometimes meaner. Every morning, when I got ready for school, buttoning my white starched shirt and tucking it into the plaid uniform skirt, I stared back into the mirror. My body had recently rounded in places that made me feel self-conscious and uncomfortable.

In the spring, after a few months of addressing my insecurities by acting loud and interrupting teachers with practical jokes, I got my first middle-school boyfriend. His name was Eric, and he had asked me at a football game if I wanted to be his girlfriend. I said yes. For three weeks, we were boyfriend and girlfriend, and we ignored each other in perfect sixth-grade fashion, until one afternoon a group of us went swimming. Eric saw me in my bathing suit for the first time and he also saw the large café au lait birthmark I have on my leg. He broke up with me immediately after—

and told everyone it was because of my unsightly birthmark. I was still smarting from this sixth-grade humiliation when Barbara and I arrived in Midland.

At lunchtime, we sat on our stools as Grammee cooked and Pa drifted in and out of reality. Suddenly, he stared at us and said, "Who are you?" And before we could react, he looked over at Barbara, and said, "Oh yes, you've always been the prettier one."

I knew he didn't mean it as soon as the words left his lips. I know now that he would have been more ashamed of saying this than of asking my father for a loan. But at that moment, to my vulnerable sixth-grade self, it was devastating to hear those words from a man who had shown me nothing but kindness, even when I most certainly deserved disciplining. Barbara looked over at me with hurt and sympathy in her eyes as I turned and bolted to our bedroom, to the familiar comfort of Grammee's sewing piles and the memory cabinet, where the boxes, books, and albums always stayed the same. Eventually there was a knock on the door. Barbara and Grammee had come to wipe my eyes and nudge me back to the kitchen.

That is the blunt cruelty of this disease. For years, the one memory I have wanted to erase is the memory of that last visit with Grammee and Pa in Midland.

As the days passed, we realized that Pa didn't even recognize Grammee. *Who are you?* he would ask. To hear him say that to our tiny grandmother—his wife of more than fifty years, who had held his hand as they buried three babies, and raised my mom—broke Barbara and me. We would escape to our room to compose ourselves. In the small house, we would hear our grandmother answer, repeatedly, patiently: *I am the one who loves you. Always.*

That seemed to answer everything.

Pa died the April after we turned thirteen, about three months after our dad was inaugurated governor of Texas. It signaled the end of our Midland summers, but more than that, our Midland lives, where we could watch the world spin by, rather than the other way around.

Sweet, Sweet Fantasy

BARBARA

Having a grandfather who was once the head of the CIA sure helps foster an overactive imagination. When we were seven, we would beg Gampy to share any and all classified information he possessed about alien life, to which he would reply that we lacked the right security clearance, before ruffling our hair and telling us, his "wieners" (yes, "wieners" means "grandkids" in the Bush family lexicon), to go out and play. But for several years, we couldn't let the aliens go. We just had to know.

Before the alien phase, we were a cat family. I don't mean we had pet cats; instead, our four cats were of the human variety, all answering to our self-given cat names: Tommy Tough (Dad) and Stripes (Mom), plus the kittens, Marmalade (Jenna) and Rosebud (me). Jenna and I made up the cats, and our parents patiently played along. Ganny, an anticat woman to the core, was horrified when as little girls we'd respond only to "Kitty," or, worse, "Here, kitty, kitty." At that point, she would probably have been happy if aliens abducted her meowing granddaughters. But our cat world symbolized us as a tiny pack of four, a nuclear family that always wanted to be together.

Like so many things in our lives, our imaginations began to form in Midland.

When we were just past being toddlers, on rare snowy nights we would venture out after dusk under the streetlights to walk with our dad. The quiet of the evening paired with the comfort of our dad made the neighborhood like our own safe snow globe. Wrapped up in our down winter coats and hoods, arms sticking out of our sides like sausages due to all of the padding, we tramped over the frozen ground. Our handsome dad would point out the glistening trees and ice-crystal lace spreading over the glass windows. We'd carry bowls and fill them with small mounds of fresh, clean snow to cover in syrup as a special winter snack, our mom telling us how snow bowls were a favorite of the pioneer children who had headed west long before we arrived. On evenings without the magic of snow, our parents read us Grimm's fairy tales—stories of fantasy and darkness that lit up our imaginations with wonder and even a touch of fear.

We left Midland, but not our fantasy life, especially Jenna, whose imagination was anything but typical and who had a flair for drama that transformed whatever home we were in. We were never bored under the dome of Jenna's expansive imagination, digging for buried treasure in our neighbor's backyard; setting up a school; or playing orphaned pioneers, two barefoot girls lost in the unexplored patches of woods amid suburban, ranch-house Dallas. Together, we would go on nature walks in the side alleys as if they were treks in the

Amazon. On hot, buggy nights, harkening back to our feline days, we howled at the summer moon. Jenna created such fantastical scenes with our dolls that Mom worried about her overactive imagination—until she read an interview with Toni Morrison's mother describing Toni's similar habits as a child.

When we were nine, Jenna sought to display her talents on a bigger stage, begging my grandmother to let her perform a solo at the Republican National Convention. Her song of choice: "Put on a Happy Face"; her costume of choice: a clown. My grandmother's firm *No* devastated Jenna. For days, she'd practice her performance over lunch, hoping she'd wow Ganny and convince her to relent. Fortunately for the sake of Jenna's ego and the convention attendees and television viewers, Ganny did not. But that did not deter Jenna from orchestrating Bush family holiday specials, where she acted as our family's director, casting me and our cousins in self-written plays. One Christmas, my dad was chosen to be the "Main Reindeer." His part consisted of ferrying our then-chubby, freckle-faced, and redheaded cousin Pierce, aka Santa, around on his back.

We never completely outgrew our imaginations. I think of Jenna and me during the 2004 election, standing at a Southwest Airlines gate, waiting to board a flight to Duluth, Minnesota. Softly, we played with the idea of dashing to the gate three doors down where the screen announced a departure to Honolulu. Or over to the international terminal where adventures to Istanbul, Singapore, and Madrid awaited. But, of course, we stuck with our campaign stop in Duluth, earning a few stares as we scanned our boarding passes and hoisted our carry-ons into the overhead bins. Aliens, perhaps, in our Boeing 737 spaceship?

Jenna was the girl who was so excited for life when we were little that she learned to crawl out of her crib and then taught and helped me crawl out of my crib every morning so we could play.

She was the girl who "took care" of the class bully when we were two on mother's day out.

She was the girl who was so imaginative and loved telling stories. I know all of y'all know about the two books that she's written, but I know ALL of the other stories she's told. Growing up, long, drawn out, dramatic stories would unfold with Jenna's Barbie and Ken.

She is a girl who has always had such a huge imagination and has always entertained me and our friends with vivid, fabulous stories.

One Valentine's Day when we were in third grade, Jenna and I were so desperate to get our ears pierced. It was all we wanted. So, the night before Valentine's Day, Jenna snuck out of our bed into the kitchen to check out the valentines that would be waiting for us the next morning. Excited, Jenna ran back into the room and told me that on the table were some sort of special pair of earrings for me that each said "Congratulations! You're getting your ears pierced." Well, I could hardly sleep all night, but the next morning we rushed into the kitchen for our presents and all I had was a measly chocolate rose.

All my life Jenna entertained me with hilarious antics like that, mainly because she wanted so badly for her stories to be true...

Mothership

JENNA

My mother was a librarian and an only child—a combination that sometimes made it hard to relate to her point of view. In her twenties, she named her cat Dewey, after the Dewey decimal system. When I was little, I was a daddy's girl. I didn't always understand my mom; more precisely, I didn't think she got me.

Growing up without a sibling made Barbara's and my antics sometimes baffling to her. When we were in high school, she hated when we let friends borrow our clothes. Nervous that we would get caught, we would sneak shirts and tops into our backpacks to give to friends who asked to borrow them for a dance or a date. They would return them in the same concealed way, inside their overnight bags when they came to spend the night. My mother told me later that she had no experience with trading or even stealing clothes as Barbara and I often did.

Solitude was an integral part of my mother's childhood. She was often alone, comforted by the beloved characters in her

SISTERS FIRST

47

books. Barbara and I had a completely different experience of childhood. Being part of a set from birth meant that we always had a playmate and that alone time was hard to come by. In moments of mischief, we enabled each other. We have the same sense of humor; when my mother scolded one of us, the other often laughed hysterically, which only encouraged more bad behavior. It was almost always two against one. We were too young and immature to consider how much my mother had wanted and wished for siblings of her own, to see how the bond between Barbara and me might have made her feel like an outsider, alone.

Barbara and I were energetic kids. My grandmother wrote as much in her memoir: "George's twins were wild. At one time they stuffed the toilet with paper, and I was up to my elbows pulling it out. I couldn't help but wonder if any other First Lady–elects had spent their morning unstuffing the toilet." But Ganny lived with our energy only in small bursts; our mom was surrounded by it every day.

Looking back now, what probably saved her, and us, was that my mom is preternaturally calm. Even in moments of panic. The night before my wedding, just as we had done countless nights before, Barbara had slept next to me in my bed. I stretched and turned to nudge her as my mom burst into the room: "Girls...wake up! Today is the day! Out of bed! Time for breakfast," she said. Then, without any drop in enthusiasm, she added, "There was a slight hiccup, but all is well. We have taken care of it!"

"What hiccup?" I asked, waking up fully.

"Oh, well, a little tornado came right through the ranch overnight. It knocked over the tent, but everything is completely fine." Only my mother could deliver the news of a tornado as if she were telling us that she had run out of toast, so we'd have to have cereal for breakfast.

Opening her eyes, Barbara laughed and asked: "Mom, are you on something to relax you?"

And the truth is, she wasn't. She is just remarkably even-tempered and able to manage everything. Strong and gentle at the same time.

She can make the best of any situation. When as girls we had to go to Atlanta to appear with Gampy when he ran for reelection, she made a big deal about it being our first trip to Georgia, and she honed in on one of our favorite pastimes: food. We are a family that loves food. We plan trips, vacations, and, yes, campaign stops around meals. She got us excited by describing the great southern food in Atlanta, especially grits and biscuits, until we could practically taste the butter melting in our mouths. But campaigns are not luxurious—when you stay somewhere, it's usually a run-down motel, which is precisely where we ended up, in a room with two double beds. I slept next to my mom, and midway through the night, one side of our bed collapsed, sending us rolling like logs toward the floor. After our crash landing, my mom, our own version of MacGyver, got up without her contacts and felt around, trying clumsily to fix the bed. She couldn't, so we slept on the slant, nearly on top of each other, for the rest of the night. And to make matters worse, the free motel breakfast had neither grits nor biscuits. The fact that I remember this story with love says everything about my mom.

As teenagers, when we would come to her with teenager-sized problems, she always said: "I promise. There are very, very few things worth worrying about." And she was right. Now, I wonder if her advice was because she had already worried about heartbreaking things and knew what it was to feel overwhelming pain. She saw our anxieties for what they were: childlike.

I think we were at the kitchen table when my mom told us about a car accident she had when she was in high school. She didn't even get to tell us in her own time and in her own way because we found out first from a comment made by one of the Texas Department of Public Safety officers on my parents' detail. She had run a stop sign in the dark and had killed the driver of the other car. The driver happened to be a boy her age, a friend. Before I knew about what had happened, I was often irritated by her constant questions and demands as we left the house: Who is driving? Don't forget a seat belt. I never suspected that her worries stemmed from an accident that still pained her more deeply than we could know. We didn't talk about it often, but the story explained a lot, and the older I got, the more I understood my mom's protective nature. She was the person who would wake each night, and ask my dad, "George, are the girls home?" Years later, she told us that she never really slept until she knew that we were back safe and in our beds.

Mother-daughter relationships can be complicated and fraught with the effects of moments from the past. My mom knew this and wanted me to know it too. On one visit home, I found an essay from the *Washington Post* by the linguistics professor Deborah Tannen that had been cut out and left on my desk. My mom, and her mom before her, loved clipping newspaper articles and cartoons from the paper to send to Barbara and me. This article was different. Above it, my mom had written a note: "Dear Benny"—I was "Benny" from the time I was a toddler; the family folklore was that when we were babies, a man approached my parents, commenting on their cute baby boys, and my parents played along, pretending our names were Benjamin and Beauregard, later shortened to Benny and Bo.

In her note, my mom confessed to doing many things that the writer of this piece had done: checking my hair, my appearance. As a teenager, I was continually annoyed by some of her requests: comb your hair; pull up your jeans (remember when low-rise jeans were a thing? It was not a good look, I can assure you!). "Your mother may assume it goes without saying that she is proud of you," Deborah Tannen wrote. "Everyone knows that. And everyone probably also notices that your bangs are obscuring your vision—and their view of your eyes. Because others won't say anything, your mother may feel it's her obligation to tell you." In leaving her note and the clipping, my mom was reminding me that she accepted me and loved me—and that there is no perfect way to be a mother. While we might have questioned some of the things our mother said, we never questioned her love.

Many times, though, my mom says the most without saying anything at all. When Barbara and I went off to college, she gave us each a photograph of her and my father as a young, newly married couple, before they had children. But it was not just any photograph. The snapshot, taken in their backyard, was given to an adoption agency after they had tried for years to conceive and had not succeeded in having a baby to love. When she handed the photo to me, my mother said, "Doesn't this just look like two people who desperately want to be parents?" I still keep the framed picture by my bed. It was her way of reminding us that we were wanted long before we were born; that to her, we came first.

My mother has never taken us for granted, and there were times when she very much wanted us to know it. The night of my wedding rehearsal dinner, she broke with tradition. Typically, the bride's mother does not speak, but my mother wanted to stand and give a toast:

When Barbara and Jenna were first born, I remember standing in the garden one night in the last few hours of light after the babies were asleep and thinking, "This is the life!" Jenna and Henry are beginning their lives together. Whatever the future holds, Jenna and Henry will continue to bring happiness and laughter into each other's lives—into all of our lives.

Twenty-six years after I stood in the garden that happy night thinking of my baby girls, I stand here with you. Tomorrow, my Jenna will stand at a beautiful altar made of the same Texas limestone that is the foundation of our home, and I will feel once more what I felt that night, many years ago: This is the life.

The backyard snapshot our parents submitted with their paperwork to an adoption agency in Texas.

Let Sleeping Vipers Lie

BARBARA

As thirteen-year-olds, we were full of angst and at times unconscionably mean to our mom. We were like so many girls that age, sharp-tongued and headstrong, and she was our most accessible target. Not to mention it was the early '90s, when teen angst was cool, worsening our mom's cause.

On the weekends, my mom would start toward our bedrooms to wake us, and my dad would shake his head and say, "No, let sleeping vipers lie." We were the vipers. And we were, to a certain degree, equal opportunity. When Ganny came for our eighth-grade graduation, she was shocked to discover that the class at our small Episcopal school's favorite movie (and ours—we saw it in the theater nine times!) was *Pulp Fiction*. Ganny loved John Travolta and sent us photos of herself and John, grinning and dancing cheek-to-cheek at the White House. Over dinner, she started to talk about the brutal violence in the film, until Jenna interrupted, "Ganny, obviously you don't understand satire." I'm sure both our parents were mortified, but Ganny was horrified. I cringe to think of what she would have said if she had seen our seventh-grade class photo, where I flipped off the photographer. (Yes, this happened.)

It all started with a small group of us standing around as we lined up by height to file into the shoot. We all decided to raise our middle fingers in unison. Classic seventh-grade mob mentality. Except I was the only one who actually did it. Some other girls held up their hands in preparation, but mine was the only one with the middle digit fully visible. It was a complete impulse and an exercise in cognitive dissonance. I never considered the consequences, but when the school enlarged the photo, made enough copies for the class, and then noticed the floating hand to my right, I had to confess. I had to march into the Episcopalian headmaster's office and apologize. My finger was airbrushed out of every photo, and I did my own penance. In the afternoons, I scraped every piece of gum off all the sidewalks around the school.

Jenna and I were not always forgiving as adolescents, but our mom forgave us for everything—well, everything except the Pearl Jam concert Jenna and I went to in Austin in eighth grade. We were allowed to go—that was not the problem. But my friend Molly and I had the inspired idea to stage dive into the mosh pit. We were sure that crowd surfing must be for us. We belonged there. Instead, it was absolutely miserable. Floating as a scrawny preteen with hundreds of sweaty hands pushing me around *hurt*. I'm not sure how my mom found out; I've always thought that Jenna told her. My three minutes of crowd surfing have haunted me for years. Every time my neck hurt after a long flight or when my muscles were sore at age thirty-five after running a half marathon, my mom chimed in: Are you sure it was from running or from the flight? Or do you think it's from the time you went crowd surfing at Pearl Jam?

Maybe it's my mom's way of saying that she had different aspirations for my musical tastes. When I was nine years old and away at summer camp, I wrote home asking for music. My friends had cassettes of New Kids on the Block. My mom sent me what could loosely be called a boy with a band: It was the box set of Bob Dylan's *At Budokan*. So while other girls were singing "Step by Step" on repeat all summer long, I was lightly humming "Simple Twist of Fate" to myself.

Lucky for us, our mom was endlessly patient. When our dad was governor, Texas Department of Public Safety (DPS) agents drove our mom around. One day, we were riding along with our mom on some now-forgotten occasion or errand. We were giving our mom a hard time almost from the moment the engine turned on. When we arrived at our destination, Jenna and I flatly refused to get out and go in with our mother. Defeated, she walked in alone. We smugly sat in the back—two vipers coiled together. The DPS agent in the driver's seat turned around. He laid into us, telling us to get out of the car that instant and go inside, adding that he expected us to apologize to her for our awful behavior. He was right. Humiliated, we did as we were told. And, of course, our sweet mama forgave us. For months afterward, Jenna and I were embarrassed and averted our eyes whenever we saw him on the detail. He'd seen us at our worst. Today, I am ashamed even to tell this story, ashamed of the way we treated our mom, who hardly ever raised her voice to us. Luckily, our thirteen-year-old attitude was short-lived.

What my mom hated most, though, was to miss any of

our events or milestones, like the time when I was crowned homecoming queen at Austin High. She knew in advance, but she had a campaign event for my dad, so she couldn't be at the football stadium that evening. Those are her regrets.

Whether in the governor's mansion or later in the White House, Mom was singularly determined to normalize our lives. Each year, she moved us into college housing and moved us out when the year ended. She bought storage bins and bed risers, and she had her own ingenious means of packing clothes. We would throw them into heavy-duty trash bags and toss them out my second-floor dorm window to the grass below. Efficient, avoiding stairs, and taking all of ten minutes to clear out a room. (I highly recommend it as a packing method.)

She doesn't use trash bags anymore, but whenever I have moved, she has been there to roll up her sleeves and help make my new apartment a home. Most of all, though, she is there, always.

On a trip to the Galápagos, my mom and I stopped to watch a baby seal roaming the beach. We realized she was searching for her missing mother, her lost love. When a pup is motherless, other seals will not take it in. This seal was calling out loudly, in a painful screech that sounded to us like, "Mother! Mother!" As I listened, I imagined just how that baby felt and so must've my mom. As she reached for my hand, our eyes welled up, and not wanting to show our tears, both of us slid on our sunglasses.

Stargazing

BARBARA

I grew up staring at the stars. On summer nights as little girls in Midland, Texas, after we had showered, my mother would hustle us into the car with our damp hair soaking the backs of our cotton nightgowns, and drive to her parents' house a few blocks away. My Grammee would be waiting for us. She would spread out a thick pink-and-baby-blue-plaid blanket on the hard, crisp grass. The air above us was hot—desert hot—even after the sun set, and the blanket below us was hot, a flannel or a brushed wool, something perfect for a winter bed. The four of us would lie side by side looking up at the clear sky, excited to be out after dark, feeling the prick of the sharp, scorched grass along our backs, listening to it crackle and break when we shifted a shoulder or stretched out a leg.

Slowly our eyes would grow accustomed to the sky and the trails of stars. And Grammee, the high school–educated, constantly learning astronomer, would point out the different constellations, the clusters of shapes made by their light. Each star was part of a story. No two stars were exactly the same. And no two continents saw the same arrangement of stars each night. Grammee would show us the closer and brighter stars and those that were older and more distant, always encouraging us to pick them out one by one. Jenna and I never learned all the constellations, but we loved the quiet beauty, the glittery magic above us as we snuggled up beside our warm and comforting mama and our grandma, who smelled of Shalimar perfume.

In eleventh grade, I secretly loved the star of the high school baseball team. Kyle was the ace pitcher for Austin High—a big deal, at least among our friends. He was handsome, unlike most awkward high school boys, and mischievous. He wasn't loud or attention-seeking, but he could make everyone laugh. We started hanging out, which for an early high school love story was the equivalent of dating. It was new and unsure, one of those shy, wobbly relationships you have when you're young. But it felt exactly like love, like a future with plans.

If you told me then that one of my friends was going to take his own life, I never would have thought to call Kyle, to ask if he was okay, to check on him.

As the school year was winding down I got mono. It was the beginning of the summer, and I was desperate to get well. I had gone from being a high schooler bursting with excitement about the promise of the vacation ahead to an ill hermit, quarantined in my over-air-conditioned bedroom. Mono made me feel exhausted, like I was living in a half-awake/half-dream state. At one point my phone rang and

Kyle's name popped up on the caller ID, but, in my fogginess, I couldn't tell if he was really calling or if my mind was playing tricks on me. Either way, I knew I couldn't be cute and funny and—using awkward teenage reasoning—I didn't want the boy I liked to hear me when I wasn't at my best, so I just listened to it ring.

I went back to sleep until Jenna came to tuck me in and tell me that our friend Sammie was having a birthday barbecue the next day. I perked up and asked, "Is Kyle going to be there?" The answer was yes. So I dozed off, sure I'd feel better by the morning. I had butterflies in my stomach in anticipation of the day to come.

The next morning, my mom woke me after I slept in. As I opened my eyes, she gently shared that Kyle had hanged himself. She didn't say that he had died. I was shocked, but I thought, *Thank God he's still alive.* He must've been found just in time; he must just be in the hospital somewhere. And so, for a minute, I believed he was still here, and I couldn't wait to get to him. And then, a few long seconds later, another devastation hit when I realized he was actually gone. Complete shock, complete confusion—how could I not have known?—followed by a complete and overwhelming sadness.

Death, particularly death when someone is so young, feels like everything is unfinished. You lose the person; you lose all your plans. I had so many daydreams, young, high school daydreams, but very real to me. We would go to prom together; we would spend the summer together. I don't daydream like that anymore.

Afterward, I tried to keep Kyle alive in my mind. Over and over, I'd listen to a voicemail from him I'd saved on my Nokia phone. He and our friend Stephen were heading out to water-ski on Lake Austin and they had invited me to come; a time when he was alive and making plans. I listened to that message until the phone's storage time expired and the voice-mails were erased. For weeks, late at night when I couldn't sleep, I'd call his number to see if he'd answer, as if this were all a huge mistake. Kyle's sister wore my prom dress to prom. It mattered to me that she wore it, because it kept me connected to him.

I went to Kyle's funeral and then to his house and afterward into his bedroom. I had never been in his bedroom before, and now there I was standing in it, but Kyle wasn't there. I looked for signs everywhere, trying to understand the boy I liked, see what I could learn about him from his belongings. To find out if we had anything else in common, if there was anything to tease him about. The same way I would have looked around if he had still been living. But he wasn't. He had hanged himself in the closet just inside that room.

After the funeral, I heard that according to the Catholic faith, if you die by suicide, you are forbidden from entering heaven. How could that be? I was so upset. Not just then, but for years after.

I am superstitious. Until I was thirty-four, every wish that I ever made, on the flame of a birthday candle or on a star, was a wish that Kyle would go to heaven. I didn't think about him every day, not the way I did in the beginning. Especially that first year, I looked up quickly in the school hallway and someone wearing the same hat he wore would walk by, and for a second I would think, *Oh, that's Kyle.* And then I would once again remember that he'd died and be devastated all over again.

The night before Easter I dreamed of Kyle. I was with him. He told me he hadn't died, that he'd just been away and that he'd "written me love letters all summer." I awoke, put on my Easter dress, and cried and cried, squeezing my abs as tight as I could—my trick to stop tears. I struggled to stay composed at church, feeling like I'd just found out the news all over again, wondering why my mind would play a trick like that, allowing me to wake and in those first few dreamy seconds believe life had been different. Gradually, those bursts of hope and devastation receded, in every way but with the stars.

Now I travel for work, often to rural places in Rwanda and Zambia where there's little electricity. From the moment the sun sets, there are stars, as bright or brighter than those Grammee and I gazed at when I was a child in Midland. When I wish on those stars, or any stars—your rare New York City star, or a star out the window of a nighttime plane—I never wish for anything other than for Kyle to go to heaven. Every birthday wish, or eyelash, or dandelion has been for Kyle. He died when I was seventeen, so by now I've made half a lifetime of wishes. But just in case it is that one additional time, that one additional wish, that makes all the others come true, I will continue to make my wishes for Kyle.

With suicide, there is no control, so I found little ways to have control. Like wishing and wishing and wishing. It began as something self-soothing—a need to believe I would see Kyle again. His place in heaven was my only chance—the only way to change the finality of his loss, a loss with no explanation. What hurt so much was that he believed he had no alternative. I longed for Kyle to be embraced in some way to somehow ease his hopelessness.

As high schoolers, my friends and I didn't know how to speak about his death. We thought we were mature, but it didn't occur to us to ask one another "How are you doing?" Too naive perhaps, too worried that compassion would cause each of us to break down, too scared to know the real answer. There was no one to talk to, no guidance counselors, not even family. Even though we were so close and I always relied on Jenna for comfort, this was the one time when I didn't know how to reach out to the ones I loved.

In February 2016, my father's good friend and partner in the Texas Rangers, Rusty Rose, killed himself. He was seventy-four, not seventeen. Rusty talked about his depression, and he defied what people thought depression is. He had a curiosity-driven, fulfilling life and he loved his kids. Dede—Rusty's wife—told the minister that she wanted his suicide acknowledged at his funeral. My dad talked about it in his eulogy. At one point, the minister said something like, "We won't brush this under the rug because people are uncomfortable. Depression is an illness. My God loves everyone. And I take that to mean that he loves Rusty, and Rusty is in heaven." It was the opposite of what I had heard before, and it was freeing.

About this same time, one of my friends suggested I go to a session with a healer. The healer asked me to gather photos of people I was close to who had passed away. My mother texted me a photo of her father, and my friend Lindsay sent one of Kyle. I didn't say anything, I didn't even tell her my name, I just showed the woman the photo. She looked at it and matter-of-factly said he had hanged himself in his closet. I started to cry, after all those years, in a recognition of having carried these memories for so long. She told me, "He has followed you everywhere, and he's so proud of all that you've done. You've been all over the world and he's gotten to go on this journey with you." Then she said, "He says you can stop counting stars now."

The thing is, I had never told anyone about my wishing. In the beginning, I didn't say anything because I was afraid that if I told someone else my wish, it wouldn't come true. Then I didn't tell anyone because it was private; it seemed like something that I shouldn't admit. Not even to my sister. The only one who might have known was handsome, funny Kyle, up there among the stars.

For most of my adult life, I've said yes to a lot of things that might sound scary, like starting a global organization. And my life has gone in directions I never could have expected back when I was young and planning my future date to the prom. Then, I thought I was going to be a fashion designer. But at a certain point I felt that I needed to do more, probably because of Kyle. I felt that if I was lucky enough to get the chance to live, I needed to take extra chances in return.

A kind man once told me that in Japan, broken pottery is pieced back together using gold as the glue, highlighting the cracks, making them beautiful. And maybe that could be my heart—hurt and healed, but filled with gold because I'd known Kyle.

Even though I may not need to, I still look up at the glittering darkness and wish on the night stars for Kyle. It is my way of reaching back to that now long-ago night and answering the phone.

Bad Math

JENNA

Barbara is a genius. I have always known it. During a preschool tryout, my architect of a sister built a block tower worthy of Frank Gehry. My contribution was to demolish it, slamming my fist into the tower until the blocks flew across the rug. My mom said the teacher gasped at our "sisterly" interaction.

No matter how much I might have wanted to be a student like Barbara, it wasn't in my nature. Our shared DNA can express itself very differently! Even when we were toddlers, my sister woke up early and went to work on our porch: drawing and coloring. I preferred physical activity, zooming around our backyard on my tricycle. Also my fine motor skills were very slow to develop. I couldn't hold a pair of scissors correctly until the third grade. At some point in elementary school, frustrated as I watched Barbara fly through work that took me far longer, I asked my mom and dad if there was something wrong with me. No, they said. We had you tested when you were younger.

I was particularly frustrated by math, a subject in which my sister excelled. In third grade, I sat in the back of Mrs. Powell's math class. Multiplication escaped me; I didn't understand the steps. (It probably didn't help that I was blind as a bat, and, without glasses, I could barely see the overhead projector.) While I was struggling to get through third-grade math, my sister placed sixth in a math competition for the entire city of Dallas. (She still has the fake gold trophy to prove it.)

I shared my mother's love of reading, but in the division of labor in the Bush household, those different parental skill sets meant my father took over math tutoring. The most obvious solution was for my dad to sit with me at the kitchen table and struggle through my homework. These evenings were not pretty; each repeated a similar pattern. My dad would patiently walk me through the steps of the math problems. But I was a resistant student, and eventually he would lose his temper. I responded by breaking into frustrated sobs, slamming my book down, and leaving the table. What neither of us could have imagined was that third-grade math would lead my dramatic self to learn what I considered a deep secret about my dad, and then to spend years of what I now know was totally unwarranted worry about my parents' marriage. (How's that for a completely unexpected answer to the vexing problem of double-digit multiplication?!)

When I received a B minus in math—my first B—my dad was disappointed, and he pushed me to do better. Always the instigator, I pushed back: *I'm sure you got a B in elementary school too, Dad.* (I had no idea that my dad was good enough with numbers to go to Harvard Business School; I didn't know what Harvard was.) My dad wasn't just going to give me his word that I was wrong, he was going to provide documentation. After a bit of hunting, he pulled out an old photo album that his mom had made for him, saving various memorabilia over the years. The dusty book was filled with report cards and black-and-white photos. He was right. He had made As.

But the scrapbook didn't end with his elementary or even high school years. On one of the pages was a tattered newspaper clipping. It was an engagement notice for George W. Bush, but the woman in the photo was young, blond, and not my mother. I looked at the man sitting next to me, my math book in his hand, and with all the indignation that my third-grade self could muster, I was outraged. How could my parents deceive Barbara and me? Math was forgotten, except for its clear connection to this terrible piece of information. Instead of doing my multiplication, I peppered my dad with endless questions, like a journalist-in-training. Was he still in love with her? Why didn't they get married? What happened to the wedding china? He patiently answered each one. He had been twenty years old. She was a college student in Texas. They were too young, and yes they had picked out a wedding china pattern.

For the next several years, my imagination was haunted by the smiling woman in the engagement photo. I was also fascinated by the fact that she had been blond, unlike my brunette mom. Disappointingly, my mom had no new information to add to my endless questions. My dad had been un-engaged for more than a decade before she met him. And she had never met his one-time fiancée.

My non-mathematically inclined mind refused to be

swayed by this new display of logic. For years, I had a re-curring dream that my parents were divorcing, broken up by the beautiful blonde. I would wake in tears and head to their room in the middle of the night, begging to sleep between them. I was well past the age of toddlers sleeping with their parents; I was a tall ten years old, but I was insistent. (It says a lot about their relationship that a child crying about their doomed marriage didn't in itself lead to a divorce!) On the plus side, it did remove math as the primary source of friction in our household.

Ten years later, Barbara and I were home from college and up late watching TV. We were about to turn off the television when a promo for *Inside Edition* came on: the President's ex-fiancée tells all. We rushed to get a VHS tape to record the interview. We couldn't wait to hear what this woman, who could've been our mother, had to say. The next morning, we woke up our dad with the tape—this was before the era of Facebook and the widespread use of Google, which has made it possible for people to easily spy on their ex-girlfriends and boyfriends. Dad gave us a slight eye roll. (He might have been happier to talk about math.)

My dad and I did have one more run-in over numbers. It was the spring of my junior year in high school, when thoughts of college dominated almost every conversation. I arrived home with some friends to discover that my sister had received her SAT scores. No surprise: She had done exceptionally well, as in she just missed one math problem! I thought to myself, *We are twins, so our scores must not be that different.* My dad knew better: *Wait until your friends leave to call and get your score, Jenna! Listen to me and wait.* Impulsivity is a weakness; plus, I firmly believed that even if I didn't do as well as Barbara, I must have scored close, right? I ignored my dad and called to get my score. (This was back in the days when you called in, rather than logged on to get your numbers.) There are five stages to SAT grief: disbelief, then denial—it must be someone else's score—then tears. Followed quickly by a somewhat humiliating exit from your friends and retreating to your room. And finally, five: the knowledge that you will be retaking the test, and signing up for SAT prep beforehand.

In the intervening years, I have had one additional revelation about math. I, too, married a man with a business school degree, and I can say with absolute certainty when either Mila or Poppy come home with a math question, the first words out of my mouth will be: "Ask your dad."

Me Without You

BARBARA

My family may seem like risk-takers, but they are even more strongly creatures of habit. My parents like to return to the same people and places year after year: Spring was Texas Rangers training camp in Florida; summer was Maine. Every one of our vacations was centered around baseball or visiting our cousins. I'm lucky to have grown up with such a tight-knit family. Still, as a teenager, I had yet to take my own adventure, and I wanted to test my limits, to figure out what I was made of and what I could do without a safety net. To be alone.

That changed the year Jenna and I turned sixteen. For each of her grandchildren's sixteenth birthdays, Ganny would take them on a trip outside the United States. It was a rite of passage—the first time we'd travel for exploration's sake, as well as the first time we'd have our grandmother all to ourselves. We were thrilled. Ganny jokingly told us she traveled in pajamas to be more comfortable on overnight flights, and our mouths dropped open in horror, our too-cool-for-school sixteen-year-old selves imagining walking through the airport with our grandmother in her PJs. Ganny showed up well dressed, and we set off for Italy, to Rome, Florence, and Venice.

Traveling with Ganny was an experience totally different from our family visits in Maine. There were not twelve other grandkids running in and out of a room. For the first time we had her undivided attention as we ate at traditional Italian restaurants, meandered through museums, or rode in gondolas along Venetian canals. We were straddling that line of childhood and adulthood, fumbling with how to act mature for our grandmother. She was impressed with our table talk about the books we were reading in high school, but terribly annoyed by our obsession with taking pictures of Italian street cats.

Because she was a former first lady, Ganny was trailed by an Italian security detail, one of whom was movie star handsome. She loved that Jenna and I would giggle and blush whenever we saw him, and we did—until he smiled back at us, revealing a mouthful of black teeth from smoking one too many cigarettes.

One of the most defining moments of my life happened when we walked down a side street near the center of Rome at midday. We stumbled upon a group of teenage students our age, clustered outside a school. They were carrying on an animated conversation that slid effortlessly from Italian, to English, to French. Scarves were tied fashionably around their necks, and bags slung over their shoulders. A few had cigarettes casually perched between their fingers. I was in awe. This was certainly not the culture at Austin High—our big public high school that felt like it was made-for-TV with the classic assortment of cheerleaders, jocks, nerds, and a marching band. It could have easily been West Beverly or Bayside High.

From the moment we boarded our return flight, I was determined to go back, and to do it soon. At sixteen, I was like a rom-com cliché of the Midwestern girl getting off the bus in New York and gazing in awe at the skyscrapers of Manhattan, or the southern girl arriving amid the swank and swagger of Los Angeles and Hollywood. I had traveled to a few other cities in the United States, but Italy was a different magnitude, and it was also a place that I happened to discover at exactly the right time in my life.

When I was very small, I thought Midland was the center of Texas and Texas was the center of everything. I couldn't imagine anyone or anything beyond this desert town, until an older man in the Dallas airport asked five-year-old me where I was from, and when I said, "Midland," he shot back a quizzical look and asked exactly where "Midland" was. That was my first clue that there was more beyond our seemingly endless horizon.

My first idea of what that "more" might be came from Grammee, who had a subscription to *National Geographic*. Grammee was curious to see the world, but because of her generation and circumstances, she did her exploring through a magazine. I sat in her Midland house and pored over the pages. I was enamored with the photographs, and my young mind began to dream of seeing the destinations in person. Then, in Mrs. Willoughby's second-grade class in suburban Dallas, we learned about the continents. When it came time for presentations, I chose Africa for my continent and Iceland for my country, imagining a land covered in glittering bluish ice, much like Narnia. I didn't simply cut out my photos and color my poster and write my sentences. I became obsessed with the concept of widely spaced continents with oceans pitching and rolling and breaking in between. I wondered what this would mean for my life, storing away the facts on languages, capitals, and populations in a deep crevice of my mind, filed under "to return to when older."

Now I had decided that I wanted to return to Rome.

I learned that the school we had seen in Rome, St. Stephen's, accepted boarders. In Austin I got my application materials together, meticulously filled out each form, and mailed them off, without asking for my parents' permission. At night, I'd dream about living in Rome: my first longing for a city, not a person. When the acceptance letter arrived, my dad remembers that I didn't so much as ask for his and my mom's approval as inform them I was going. A couple of years ago, he recalled, "How could we say no, when she had already completed everything a parent would usually do?"

Until that fall, there had never been a school year that did not start with both Jenna and me walking through the same door together. We were so in tune and so close that we met and made our friends at the same time; each of us had a constant companion during those unfamiliar experiences that give most kids sweat-inducing anxiety. Yet now I wanted to try separation. Let me explain: I was three years old and it was Halloween. Jenna was dressed as a clown, and I was a star baby. In the grainy home video, my dad panned the camera to me and asked, "What's your name, little girl?" Before I could even open my mouth to answer, Jenna jumped in front of me for center-stage position. My constant sidekick sure made life fun, but I was eager to find my own voice. To stand alone. Rome would be my test.

The flight itself was almost a disaster. I was ticketed from Dallas to Rome, with a stopover in Frankfurt, Germany. When the plane landed, I got off, but I couldn't make sense of the German signs—*eingang, tor, ausfahrt.* Too shy to ask for help until the last minute, I wandered the airport holding back tears, almost missing my connection. Half tempted to turn around and go home, I was worried that I lacked the bravery to attend school in another country. When I finally landed in Rome, I was too scrawny to pull my heavy bag off the conveyor belt in baggage claim. Thankfully, another passenger hauled it off after watching me struggle, fail, and then chase it as it rotated around, my heart beating furiously. Unbeknownst to me, with that fear I was falling in love. In love with being scared and unsure; in love with being far outside my comfort zone.

In Rome, everything was different; even the ordinary seemed grander. The school was housed inside a cavernous former convent near the Circo Massimo and the Colosseum. The countries that were once dollops of color on a pull-down map in my tenth-grade geography class came to life via newly made school friends from Kuwait, Chad, and Japan. My roommate, and soon-to-be best friend, was Josefine—a six-foot-tall brown-haired girl from Sweden. She wore all black with bright white Superga sneakers (always bright white—I'm still not sure how she kept them so clean), forecasting a trend that would arrive in the United States a decade later. Très European. We were free to wander the Spanish Steps and Trastevere until our 7 p.m. weekday curfew. Josefine and I would jog throughout the old city, listening to mixtapes we'd made for each other of Ani DiFranco on our bright yellow

Sony Walkmans. We'd do our homework in the orangerie out-side Casa Borghese. Bold Italian teenage boys would chase after us and scream out *"Americana! Americana!"* We would meet friends for coffee at our local bar (I'd never touched cof-fee in Texas), ride around on the back of *motos* to go watch *fútbol* games, or take buses across Rome.

After years of riding around in the backseats of cars in Texas, I adored public transportation. I was so enthralled with the bus that I'd often miss my stop or get lost down a back alley. Kind bus drivers would arrive at the end of their route with me still dreamily gazing out the window in the back. In broken English they'd tell me I'd ridden too far. I would rush to get home before curfew (often not making it), se-cretly adoring the romantic experience of getting lost and the adrenaline rush of having to navigate my way back before the school gates closed.

Josefine and I took the train across the country to visit our friend Orlando's family in Tuscany. We wandered through fields and vineyards and ate huge Italian meals, while pantomiming conversations with his non-English-speaking *nonna*. After a long weekend of wine and beauty, we both fell asleep on our train back from Tuscany, only to be awakened by an Italian conductor who also did not speak English. Words were lost in translation, but it was clear we were no longer meant to be on the train. Without the train ever coming to a halt, he hoisted our bags up and threw them out the door; we jumped off, following them into a field, and turned around to see a smiling conductor shout-ing, *"Grazie, bellas,"* as he shrank farther into the distance.

Josefine and I were emboldened by our newfound sense of independence. Perhaps a little too emboldened. We would hitchhike across Rome to make curfew—just two sixteen-year-old girls putting their lives in the hands of complete strangers to avoid getting into trouble with our school. We worked out a fail-proof system: We'd hail down a driver, pile into the car, and pull out a disposable camera. The unsuspecting driver would turn around to a flash in his eyes before he drove his English-speaking cargo down the road. With a photo of our driver, we were sure nothing could go wrong. And, luckily for us, nothing did.

Words of wisdom: Always photograph your hitcher.

Rome was the first place I created an identity apart from my sister. When roll was called, I was the only one named "Bush" on the roster. In an era before widespread e-mail and Internet, our only link was a two-hour nightly window when I could use the shared phone in the dorm hallway, the same two hours that Jenna was in class in Austin High. We talked in snippets, and, for a few months, our lives diverged. It made us independent. When we were together again after that, it felt like a choice, not a habit or even an obligation. Our bond was better, stronger, and more sure.

Yet my life in Rome became more real once Jenna could experience it alongside me. When she and my parents came for an Italian Thanksgiving, she met my new friends and wandered the streets, she tasted steaming pizza from our favorite pizza cart, and she heard the echo of her own feet through the dining hall. She could meet my Italian boyfriend, who wondered about this so-called "twin" of mine. (Note to men around the world: Do not arrive late to meet a Texas girl's father because you are buying flowers. This will not win him over. Nor will it win her over.)

As much as I missed her, Rome also gave me the confidence that I could be part of a wider world.

Years later, I did go back to Rome with my mom, as a stopover on the way to the 2006 Winter Olympics in Turin, Italy. But as lovely as it was, it wasn't the same as my private Rome in high school. A walk to the Spanish Steps required four Secret Service agents and four Italian security agents. People turned around to look, wondering who the famous person they didn't recognize was. On one particular day, instead of going out to sample the street pizza, I was invited to a private tea with Pope Benedict. Everything was rigidly preset, right down to the specific minutes allowed for the courtesy gift exchange.

It was memorable, surreal even, but it also made me eager for the chance to once again explore the world alone, as just Barbara.

Happy Valentine's Day
An ode to da sista

Roses are Red
I have a big head!
You and Jay may wed…
I may be dead
Let's go to Club Med
Ganny loves Keds
My heart is red
YOU ARE THE BEST SISTER
FROM HERE TO MADRID!!

—Jenna

You Win Some, You Lo(o)se Some

JENNA

At the start of 1992, in my loopy, oversized fourth-grade hand-writing, I wrote a short entry in my turquoise faux-vinyl diary listing my most pressing New Year's resolutions: "loose four pounds and join the Preston Hollow Elementary student council." ("Loose"? Maybe one of my resolutions should have been to practice my spelling!) The election was months away, and yet I wanted to win it with that great rush of single-minded focus. (I also told my diary that I would be writing entries only on the weekends.)

Perhaps I thought of elections as a family business or I wanted to please my parents. Or maybe I thought the position would make me popular. Or I just wanted to be on the student council in the same way that I wanted a perm because I didn't like my straight, uninteresting hair.

This being Texas, where everything is always bigger, our elementary school election wasn't about simply making cute posters and casting a vote during morning meeting. Each candidate had to have a running mate and a costume and make a speech in front of the school. I picked a fifth-grade girl as my running mate, thinking that an older partner would give me an advantage, and my costume was Uncle Sam, with the slogan "I want you to vote for me." My platform was about school lunches and bake sales, which might also have related back to those four extra pounds.

I thought the speech went well, and then we got the results: I had lost to a beautiful sixth-grade girl.

I came home and wedged myself into the tiniest, darkest place I could find: a crawl space under our rear patio where all the watering apparatus lay tucked away. I lay down on the dirt floor, amid the leaves and bugs, and cried. Eventually, my mom and Barbara came outside and peered in—it would have been too early for my dad to be home, although he had the most experience with losing. His marriage to my mom began with a failed run for Congress in West Texas. My mom, in her calm, soothing way, talked about how it was almost a certainty that the older girl would win, and how there was always next year.

It was years before I considered running for school office again.

There were plenty of other Bushes up for election. Just a few months later, my grandfather, our Gampy, would lose his race to be reelected president. I don't recall much about the campaign, except for one afternoon after my mother had finally given in and allowed me to get a perm. She drove me out to the Regis Salon, located inside a sprawling Dallas mall off one of the city's big expressways. I remember the heavy black cape draped over me and the anticipation as the stylist pumped up the chair. I was so overjoyed by the smell of the putrid chemicals and their sting on my scalp, promising lush blond waves and large hair, that at first the red, white, and blue Ross Perot campaign button pinned to the stylist's denim jacket barely registered. It was only when I looked over at my mom and noticed how rigidly she sat, clenching a magazine she was barely reading, that the full connection sparked. The pin stared back at me in the mirror. Ross Perot was the Texas oilman running as a third-party candidate against Gampy, who was in turn campaigning against both Ross Perot and Bill Clinton. Suddenly, some of the magic disappeared from this long anticipated day.

There are many breathless moments when your loved ones run for political office. We spent November's presidential Election Day in Houston, swimming in the hotel pool and eating an early pizza dinner with our cousins, but deep down, we felt the gravity of the situation. The next morning, it was like an existential death, where there was no wake or funeral, but the adults walked around grim. I remember my dad with tears in his eyes. Then two years later, my father ran and won his race for governor of Texas. In the spring of 1999, he sat Barbara and me down on the brick patio of the governor's mansion in Austin and said, "I'm going to run for president, and I want your approval."

There was no crawl space then.

Diary Entry 5/2/96

Today has been a hard day for me. This morning there was a picture of Me + Barbara in the newspaper—and an article—on us going to AHS—how dumb is that? There are 1000 freshman going to AHS so what makes us special—my last name—how unfair is that? The thing that really sucks is I'll be known for "Jenna Bush" the thing instead of Jenna Bush the person. I'll be known as the Governor's Daughter—not as who I am. There are a lot of people at AHS + I know I won't be friends w/ all of them so even by the time I graduate, to some of those unknown faces I'll still be known as the governor's daughter. I know it's not my parents' fault but I'm taking it out on them because there is not anyone else to blame—and I always have to blame someone! Also—being the Gov. Daughter stereotypes me as a rich, snobby bitch—so I think people at AHS think that. I've had a horrible week—my best friend Kate and I have had some trouble—or we're not that close—she is spending a lot of time w/ this girl named Bridget. I <3 Bridget too. But it's hard not to get jealous—I feel like I'm losing her. I'm glad the wk. ends here, almost. School is almost out—I'm so sad but I can't wait until summer—at least you will know me for the real "Jenna Bush."

Despite the feelings in my journal entry, Barbara and I lived normal lives, even as the governor's children. We had our driver's licenses and an old, slightly beat-up Jeep that we shared to drive to Austin High School, where we were two of about twenty-five hundred. We knew all of that would change. We tried to lobby my dad not to run for president, the way we did to go to a school party or to be allowed to drive the car somewhere, thinking if we made our case persuasively enough, he might cave, because occasionally he did. But not this time. His desire to serve was not going to be undone by our teenage angst. (In retrospect, I can see how naive we were, not appreciating that we would truly get to live history.) When we went off to college, our parents were on the campaign trail. Your life changes once you become presidential children. By second semester, we had Secret Service following behind us. Our faces were on the covers of magazines and the front pages of newspapers. People knew who we were; it felt like there was a spotlight illuminating us. We traveled under fake names, like Barbara's Holly Crawford (which sounded vaguely like an exotic dancer); and mine, the much blander Sarah Jackson, so if anyone got ahold of a passenger list or a hotel registration, we would be all but impossible to find. Even just walking out of a dorm, anything could happen. Someone could say something that would break our hearts. The first couple of years of my dad's presidency, I felt nervous to be alone; I didn't want to go to class by myself. I took huge introductory classes so I wouldn't have to sit in a small circle around a seminar table and say my name. It wasn't until about junior year that I finally started to feel safer in my own skin.

At first, we were unsure on how to be presidential children. But we found out quickly that as awkward as our new role was, it gave us the world. We traveled to Africa and Europe, met heads of state and kings and queens, and had a front-row seat to an entire decade simply by being born.

And then, of course, ironically, it would be during my dad's reelection campaign that I would meet the love of my life and my future husband. But that is a new story for another page.

BARBARA

I ran for treasurer of the student council the same year Jenna ran for vice president. I chose a fifth-grade boy as my running mate, a daring move, as talking to older boys wasn't something fourth-grade girls did. My teacher, Ms. Flowers, had thoughtfully suggested it—broadening our "ticket" to both genders and two grades. Strategic. Unlike many others in my family, I lacked any innate political instincts and was very much in need of her outside consulting.

I didn't care all that much about the actual election. I was mostly interested in the crafts that could accompany a campaign. I liked making campaign buttons, and I was particularly excited about my costume. Yes, my sister and I felt it appropriate to dress up for our one political foray. Our theme was the tortoise and the hare: I dressed up as a turtle; my running mate, the hare. My mother's friend Pam, a professional artist, helped me make my own turtle shell—it was textured, it was rhinestoned, it was a Texas hot-glue-gun dream. The only problem was, the shell looked best from behind. When practicing my speech in front of my mom, I struggled with how to show it off in all its glory. I had to incorporate a turn. The moment I fell silent with my back to the audience was the highlight of my speech; I was genuinely terrified about speaking to the entire school.

When it came time to vote, I marked the ballot for all of my friends. It didn't occur to me to vote for myself. When I told my parents, they smiled and said, "Well, that's why you lost."

Some eight years passed before the next consequential election, and the first one in which Jenna and I could vote. We had turned eighteen during our dad's campaign, so my ballot for him was the first I'd ever cast. Rather than dressing up and heading to the polls, I was away at school and mailed in my absentee ballot. No "I Voted" sticker, but I was proud nonetheless.

For election night in November 2000, I flew to Texas from New Haven, Connecticut, where I was in college at Yale. My first flight out was canceled due to weather, and I was panicked I wouldn't make it back in time and would have to watch the results on the terminal's TV. Luckily plane number two took off for Austin. A family dinner was planned—grandparents, uncles, aunts, and cousins all flying in to wait for the results. We gathered at the Shoreline Grill, just a few blocks from where, win or lose, my dad and our family would take the stage for him to speak. We cloistered ourselves away in a private back room blocked off by thick velvet curtains. It was as if our Maine dining room had been transported to Texas, except instead of shorts and relaxed beachwear everyone was dressed up and our typically high-energy crew was even more energized.

As usual, Jenna and I sat at the "kids'" table, excited to ditch the adults and catch up with our cousins, who wanted to know everything about life in college; for our part, we were curious about our cousin Sam's new girlfriend. There was an underlying tension, but we cracked jokes to ease it. We hardly even spoke about why we were gathered—we had no control at that point, so it was better to adopt a Zen Buddhist approach to the whole evening—though we'd regularly glance at our dad, who was quietly entertaining his siblings and parents and flashing his easy smile. As a family, we had been through two other presidential elections, one that ended in victory, and the most recent one, which had ended in defeat. We knew from Gampy's election nights that either outcome would be okay for our family, that we would get up in the morning and life would go on, but that knowledge didn't dull the buzzing sense of anticipation.

The year 2000 was just on the cusp of widespread cell phone use, so only a few people's pockets rang, while the multiline stand-alone phones on a side table blinked and trilled. It seems foreign now, when most of the world vibrates or chimes with texts, but Jenna and I were not connected. The room only started crackling when there was a personal update. As voting ended, Karl Rove ran in and out, sharing information about exit polls and early returns. Jenna and I made small talk to pass the time, but it gradually became unfocused, the kind where you drop your train of thought because your mind has veered off onto other things. Some moments, we'd be celebrating and hugging our dad, and then with the breathless delivery of another piece of news, we would retreat to our chairs.

Dinner—parmesan-crusted chicken—was just being served when NBC called Florida for Al Gore (meaning my dad would likely lose), and my parents quietly left for the privacy of the governor's mansion. It was almost unnoticed; no formal good-bye, but rather the hosts slipping out so as not to cut the dinner short or ruin everyone else's evening: an Irish Exit. Uncle Jeb and my grandparents soon followed. We stayed behind and ate a bit more. Realizing that the governor's mansion apartment was tiny and would be packed with political adults, we retreated to our cousins' hotel rooms. The only thing we knew was that everyone, from the media to both campaigns, was confused.

Riding the hotel elevator felt like we were part of a Super
Bowl team down by one point at halftime, escaping the thun-
derous stadium for the seclusion of an underground tunnel.
But we assumed that within a few hours, the anticipation and
the uncertainty would end. The United States would have a
new president. Then the networks retracted their calls for Al
Gore, and the momentum swung again.

Jenna and I ended up lying in our cousin Wendy's hotel
bed watching the news and saying next to nothing. Florida
was going back and forth. After 1 a.m., Florida was put into
the "Bush column," and Al Gore called to concede. Our parents phoned, telling us to get ready so we could be onstage
when Dad accepted the presidency. We jumped up, got out
of our dress clothes, put on bathrobes, and started freshening
our makeup and ironing to look presentable, rather than
smudged and wrinkled, for the cameras and the crowd. An
hour later, Vice President Gore called back and retracted his
concession. It was now close to three in the morning. Jenna
and I headed home. The governor's mansion was empty and
the lights had been turned off; our parents were waiting up
in their PJs ready for bed. It was just like any other night—
no hysterics—we just didn't know who had won. They kissed
us good night and we fell asleep down the hall, hopeful that
by later that day we'd have an answer. When we woke, nothing had been decided. There was going to be a recount, even
though Jenna and I didn't know exactly what that would
mean.

Jenna and my parents stayed behind in Austin, but I got on
a plane back to New Haven in anticipation of my first college
exams, uncertain and completely alone.

Now we live in an era of twenty-four-hour news cycles and breaking news alerts, but I can't remember ever having a political discussion with my high school friends twenty years ago. We would bring in our carefully clipped newspaper articles and discuss current events in class. I was often passionate about a particular event because, as a human, I wanted to make the world better. But our discussions were never heated or intense or partisan. When we left the class, it was over. We were focused on the minutiae of high school: school dramas and school lives. Even at the governor's mansion, my dad rarely discussed politics at the dinner table; like a doctor, lawyer, or business owner, he wanted to unwind with his family, not bring work home. We were far more likely to hear a passionate exchange about the Texas Rangers, or questions about our day at school, my parents digging deeper when we would reply with the standard, "It was fine."

So I was unnerved to discover that Yale was the opposite, a very political campus. Intellectually, I knew it would be, but emotionally, I was unprepared. The students living in the dorm across from mine had Al Gore signs in all their windows. I couldn't look out my window without seeing one. The only way to avoid them was to stare at the ground. I knew the signs were not personal, but it still felt like a stab each time I saw one, because for me it was unavoidably personal. It was Bush versus Gore; my dad versus another man. Who would be a better president? Who was more worthy? The person on the other side of the recount was my father.

I specifically chose to go to a school where I didn't know a single person, wanting to meet new people and "broaden my horizons" (whatever that meant to an eighteen-year-old). Once the recount started, I wondered if that was the right choice. At Yale, everyone walked everywhere. All of a sudden, I could feel people looking at me. Their heads would twist or they would stare just a little too long. I was grateful so many other kids on campus were a bigger deal. Claire Danes, the actress, was a Yale student, and she was much more exciting to spot than me. I don't know if I made it easier or harder to adapt by averting my eyes and staring down at the ground as I walked.

Nevertheless, the election and the recount were hot topics, as I'm sure they were on most campuses. Students were respectful if I was around, but they were also humans sharing their political beliefs. I didn't, however, hear anyone stand up for my dad. Instead, I listened to people accusing him of stealing an election. To me, though, these were not just abstract discussions; they were talking about my father, someone I loved. My heart cracked a tiny bit at each comment, thinking of my dad, who called every week eager for details about my life at Yale, picturing me where he had happily spent four years.

In many ways, I was fortunate that it was the year 2000. These were the last days of dry-erase message boards on dorm room doors, where people left notes when they dropped by rather than sending texts from down the hall. There was no Facebook, no Twitter; whatever my friends might have thought or said when I wasn't around, I never saw them post anything. Few students had cars on campus, so there were no bumper stickers to advertise their political beliefs. The only way to start a protest was to tack flyers to lampposts and entryways.

As the recount dragged on, I became quiet, silent behind a smile when I was with strangers. A humanities professor invited me to see him during his office hours. He wanted to know why I barely spoke in his seminar. In high school, I had always been an eager participant, confident in myself, in my questions and answers. I was embarrassed that he had called me in and pretended everything was fine, telling him that I was just a soft-spoken student. But he kindly prodded. For the first time with anyone at Yale, I acknowledged my dad might become president. In a seminar of twelve, it seemed as if any word I uttered was suddenly loaded. I didn't want to have every phrase dissected by eleven other students. I didn't want to be second-guessing everything that I might say. I didn't want to call attention to myself.

I had the sweetest roommates. As a freshman, I was matched up with three other girls I didn't know. We lived in a two-bedroom dorm containing two sets of bunk beds. I have no idea who they voted for; we never talked about it. Perhaps this would be a very different chapter if I'd had different roommates. In many ways, they were my own Secret Service—always loyal and protective. Looking back on it, I wonder if they helped me avoid some of the commotion. They'd usher me out of a party, claiming they were tired, if someone pulled out a bulky digital camera and pointed it in my direction. Off we'd go, arm in arm; they played the role of the ones needing me as an escort, when secretly I knew it was for my own sake. Were there protest marches on one street when they took me down another? Hallways with certain anti-Dad posters that they made sure I avoided? Sometimes friendship is about opening your eyes to new places; sometimes it's about making sure that you don't see too much.

Throughout the recount and for years after, I became a turtle of sorts, a hard shell of self-protection over vulnerable love.

I was studying for finals when my parents called me on a Tuesday to tell me about the Supreme Court decision that ended the recount and awarded Florida's electoral votes to my dad, making him the forty-third president of the United States. He went on television that night from Austin to give his acceptance speech from a podium in the statehouse, asking everyone to move on from the uncertainty, the divisiveness. I don't remember if I watched or if I was completely absorbed in my studies.

I returned to Austin to spend one last Christmas in my childhood home, the governor's mansion, where Jenna and I had lived since we were thirteen. Packing boxes were stacked in corners; my parents were moving to DC. I went to bed at night knowing that I would never be coming back to my bedroom.

The last day I spent at home was also my first day of Secret Service protection. I met Steve, a thirty-six-year-old father and the new head of my security detail, as we got into the car to drive to the airport after I turned around for one last good-bye. Steve says that at the time he thought I was quiet; but I was likely sullen, unaware of what lay around the bend.

Upstairs at 1600

JENNA

People ask us all the time: What was it like to live in the White House? I certainly didn't believe in ghosts before we moved into the White House; nor did I imagine that people who were strangers when we met could end up feeling so much like family.

When I think about the White House as a place, one image always returns to my mind. As children, Barbara and I were in love with a dollhouse shop in Maine. The store itself was located inside an old gabled Victorian house, and once a summer our mother would take us there to wander among the beautifully created miniatures of classic Cape Cod and Victorian houses. We would stop at each one, open the roofs, and peer into the rooms filled with shrunken antique furniture, so different from our one-story ranch home in Dallas. (One year for Christmas, Santa gave each of us an unfinished dollhouse to decorate. Although we played with them often, our houses remained construction zones. To this day, they sit unfinished in Texas. My mom now promises she will complete them for my girls.)

Walking into the White House for the first time when my grandfather was elected president felt like stepping into a very elaborate, fully completed dollhouse. The antique furniture was so similar to the tiny doll furniture that had enchanted us in Maine. Everything was formal, except for the hallways and passageways. There, with our cousins, we played epic games of hide-and-seek in the alcoves and stairwells and spent hours competing in contests of "slide down the back banisters."

Our first weekend visiting, Barbara and I went down to the single-lane bowling alley in the basement and used the big phone to call up to the kitchen and request two peanut butter and jelly sandwiches. We were like Eloise in our own Plaza! When the door opened, it was not our sandwiches, but our Ganny, who appeared and told us in no uncertain terms that we were not in a hotel, but temporary guests in a historic home, and we were never to do that again. We never did.

We did understand, too, even at an early age, that a house is not automatically a *home*. Living in the White House is time-limited; a family has four or at the most eight years within its walls. Everything is temporary; even most of the White House furniture is stored in warehouses and you are merely borrowing it from the country. (Our personal furniture was moved to my parents' ranch, and all my mom brought with her was a chest of drawers.) What made the space a home were the people, past and present. The people who worked at the White House became a second family to us. They turned what could feel like a cold museum into a place filled with life.

Our greeter as seven-year-olds at our grandfather's inauguration was Nancy, the White House florist, who ushered us in from the cold. She helped us make colorful bouquets of winter flowers to place at our grandparents' bedside for their first night under this historic roof. Twenty years later, I could see the love she poured into every gorgeous bouquet that she created for my wedding.

Every morning, Buddy and Ramsey, two of the White House butlers, were the first people we saw when we walked into the family dining room to eat our oatmeal, which they carried in. Their presence was what warmed that very formal room, where the dark, carved-wood chairs were stiff and the glossy table was unbearably fancy. When Gampy was president, they had played games with us. Now that my dad was president, they were our friends. We knew that Buddy was a die-hard Dallas Cowboys fan who rode his Harley to work. Every week, Ramsey brought magazines for my mom to read, and if there was an article about her, he marked the exact location with a Post-it note. With Barbara and me, he talked about his many girlfriends. When I brought Henry around, Ramsey said to him, "We love this girl. Take good care of this girl."

Because we were away at school, we visited the White House only for holidays and school breaks. When we did come home, Barbara and I slept in the same side-by-side bedrooms that Caroline and John Kennedy Jr. had occupied before us and Malia and Sasha Obama would after. My mother put out silver picture frames filled with our baby photos and photos of college friends and boyfriends. She also had two queen beds placed in each of our rooms, with the hopes that we would return often and bring our friends.

We did invite our friends, and we tried to embrace the

old times, literally. Every year around July 4, Barbara and I would host an olden-times party, where each guest had to come in costume as a historical figure. One year, I was Martha Washington. The next year, Barbara and I went as a pair of saber-toothed tigers. (What's older than prehistoric cats?) One butler's cousin was a DJ, and he provided the music for the party. "Martha Washington" and "Davy Crockett" danced to the sounds of OutKast and 50 Cent in the East Room. Barbara and I invented a move we called the "Bucking Bronco" where I rode Barbara across the dance floor like a horse.

We were always nervous that someone might break a glass or the fancy White House china, but fortunately for us, our guests were probably more intimidated than we were. The only party "foul" occurred at a Christmas get-together when one of our guests tried to leave with a tree ornament hidden in his hand. The Secret Service agents manning the door stopped him. He was reprimanded and removed—and the ornament returned. (Stealing things from the White House is, sadly, pretty common. For years, guests have taken place-card holders, silverware, even printed towels from the bathrooms. My mom always rolls her eyes slightly when she recalls how one very well-known journalist would stuff her bag with official towels every time she went to the ladies' room!)

Our favorite party of the entire year was the staff Christmas party, when the men and women who worked there brought their families and were the guests. No matter where we were, Barbara and I tried to return for that evening. Our saddest day was the tea on the morning of President Obama's inauguration, when everyone who worked at the residence said good-bye. We hugged every single person in the room: Dale, the grounds expert who also looked after Barney, Beasley, and

Spot; Bill, the dessert chef who baked the best White House cookies; and Cris, the head chef, whose food and smile lit up the house.

Not long after my dad left office, one of the loveliest butlers, appropriately nicknamed Smiley, passed away. Smiley was a cheerleader for everyone, always encouraging, and known for having an endless supply of hugs. Barbara, my mom, and I went back to Washington for his funeral. We sat in our pew sobbing over the loss of this lovely man who had been such a part of our lives. Mrs. Obama was there, too, and, a few years later, she mentioned to me that she didn't completely understand at the time why we were so upset at Smiley's passing, but now she did. She said that the men and women in the residence had become like family to Malia and Sasha as well, which prompted me to recall that one of the best afternoons Barbara and I spent in the White House was when we showed Malia and Sasha around what was soon to be their new home.

While the White House is perhaps the most public house in the world, at the same time it is one of the most private. It is a house that has seen so much; the more nights you spend there, the more you wonder about what happened before.

One summer night after my junior year of college, I had gone to sleep until my phone rang with a late-night call from a friend in Texas. As I closed my eyes again, I heard sounds coming from the fireplace in my room. I shot bolt upright in bed. I could distinctly hear a female opera singer's voice ringing from the fireplace, I ran into Barbara's room, slipping on the glossy wooden floors. I leaped into her bed and woke her, exclaiming, "Sissy, there was opera singing coming from my fireplace! I have goose bumps all over my legs. Sissy!"

My practical sister simply said, "Okay," and added that it was probably just someone listening to music somewhere else in the house. She told me to go back to sleep. As Barbara drifted off, I lay there, wide awake, slowly talking myself out of what I had heard. Barbara must have been right. It must have been someone working upstairs and listening to music. Did workers spend the night in the White House?

Several nights later, Barbara was sleeping in my room. After we turned off the lights, we talked quietly for a few minutes. Then we both heard it: 1920s piano music streaming from the same fireplace in my room. This time Barbara was the one who jumped out of her bed and ran into mine, her heart pounding. "What was that?"

We knew that if anyplace was haunted, it was this house, but we tried to rationalize it. Maybe it was Willard, our cat, walking across the piano in the hallway. The next morning, I saw Buddy as we walked out of my room, and I noticed that the piano cover was down. It couldn't have been Willard, and if it had been, she would have become some sort of Internet sensation, playing jazz piano with her paws.

"How did you sleep?" Buddy asked.

"Not great," I replied. Then I explained about the eerie piano music and the opera singer I had heard the week before. "It sounds crazy, I know," I said.

"Oh, Ms. Jenna, I believe you. You wouldn't believe what I have seen and heard over the years." Buddy hasn't yet told me his ghost stories, but I keep hoping.

Today, all I have of the White House are my memories, including my first kiss with Henry, which was up on the third-floor balcony overlooking the South Lawn, the same place where President Dwight Eisenhower liked to make steaks on a tiny grill. Whenever I see a shot of those white pillars and fountains, I always linger on it an extra second, still faintly feeling the pulse of all those other families who have lived there, with their secrets, stories, and memories—and now ours, too—that have seeped into the foundation, to forever be a part of the house itself.

Code Name: Turquoise

BARBARA

For more than eight years, until I was twenty-seven years old, someone, or rather, many someones, always knew where I was. I could never casually saunter across Yale's sprawling campus or walk down a New York street, or even walk along a hard-packed dirt path in rural Texas and not glance over my shoulder to see familiar faces trailing me. The perpetual helicoptering meant that any carefree and impulsive road trip with friends to Myrtle Beach—which I did one year with a group of girlfriends—was followed by a requisite tail of brooding black Expeditions. Not even a lane could be changed without an exact copycat movement by my Secret Service. The adage that warns, "Never drive faster than your guardian angels can fly," took on profound meaning for my driver friends because they actually *couldn't* drive faster than my Secret Service angels could fly or drive.

I was not fully aware of all the ways they watched over

and watched out for me. They intercepted my mail and read it first, so that I never received a nasty or threatening note. If someone lingered too long at my entryway or later at my apartment door, an agent appeared and suggested that the person move on. After I was no longer under Secret Service watch, I had my share of stalkers, strange people who repeatedly turned up on my doorstep. I learned to walk down the other side of the street on my way home so I could see from a distance if someone was already standing on my doorstep, waiting. It was scary at age thirty. There is no way I could have handled these incidents at nineteen or twenty-one, and I will always be grateful to have had my protectors. In the same breath, though, there was also something a bit unnatural about other people knowing every detail of my life, and me knowing so little of theirs.

My agents lived a dual life—"living" mine along with me (from a distance) and also living their own lives when they returned to their wives and husbands and homes during off-duty hours. Yet they would still be debriefed on my every move—they knew if I spent the night out and wasn't coming home until the next morning, and if I made a late-night run to a diner for pizza. I would even bet they knew who my crush was. It was a bizarre type of comfort that they fishbowled my life without judgment.

It could not have been easy for my detail. Most people living under Secret Service protection—dignitaries, presidents, officials, actual *adults*—go to offices and have predictable schedules. I was an eighteen-year-old college student, so my schedule was about as predictable as the motions of asteroids. The agents in cargo pants and heavy jackets, waiting for me in all weather conditions and at all hours of the day and night, were not in the forefront (or even the back) of my mind. I couldn't tell them in advance where I'd be studying or when, or where I'd be going at night, so they spent a lot of time just keeping up.

Steve, who headed my detail for years, has joked that I was the most protected girl on the Yale campus; and my roommate, Laura, "was the second most protected girl." Laura and I both had long brown hair, we both had blue eyes, and we both had the same black North Face jacket. And we were both habitually late to class, darting out of the same dorm room entryway at a dead run. The agents would see a brown-haired, black-jacketed girl dash by and they would start sprinting to "get a visual." If it was Laura, they stopped moving, but if it was me, they continued the chase.

After 9/11, I traveled under a fake name: Holly Crawford, so that if anyone looked at a passenger manifest they wouldn't see "Barbara Bush" and know which plane I had boarded. Early on, Steve and I took a Southwest flight out of Austin. We'd gone through security unnoticed (several men revealing their guns), and "Holly Crawford" slid onto the plane. It was smooth and completely natural; no one recognized me, but then Steve looked over and saw that I had taken off my shoes and was sitting with my socked feet showing. My crossed legs exposed the underside of my white socks, where my mother had diligently written "B. Bush" in permanent marker before I went to camp. My socks were a more blatant advertisement of my identity than any boarding pass. Busted. Steve groaned and whispered to me to put my shoes back on.

It was my agents' particular bad luck that I chose to attend a college that was also a major tourist destination. Sightseeing buses would pull up and discharge throngs of visitors with telephoto lenses, eager to explore the third-oldest university in the United States. Architecture students sought out the many distinctive buildings on campus, including Davenport College, which happened to be my residential dorm. Yale is a small place, and it was easy to discover that I lived in Davenport. My agents used to sit on a bench in the courtyard, pretending to read, while their eyes darted back and forth, watching for anyone with a camera. After a few clicks of the shutter, an agent would approach and ask the person why they were taking pictures and insist upon seeing the photos. I was mortified, but to my question of "Do you really have to do this?" they would reply, "We just don't know how it could be used."

I understood this safety measure after Saddam Hussein's sons Uday and Qusay were killed in June 2003. Uday's personal zoo held lions, cheetahs, and a bear; the storehouse next to his home held $1.65 million worth of fine wines and liquors, as well as heroin. He was known as a rapist, prone to "homicidal rages," and was even called a serial killer by some. Among his public displays of violence, he shot and killed an army officer whom he accused of flirting with his wife, and he beat his father's valet to death in front of a crowd of partygoers. He and his brother were best known inside Iraq for overseeing the killing of their father's political opponents. Uday's house was stocked with Cuban cigars and cases of champagne; and, plastered on the walls of the brothers' gym, American troops found photos of Jenna and me. Our images were scattered among hundreds of photos of naked women— "the biggest collection of naked women I'd ever seen," according to US Army captain Ed Ballanco, who added that it "looked like something at the Playboy Mansion." (Even though we were clothed, the news was terrifying as the gravity of it sank in.) It was chilling. Suddenly, I needed to be worried for myself in a way I had never imagined. The "threats" I understood intellectually had become real. Steve was even more worried. For an extended period, he barely left my side.

I can't say whether we would have spent so much time in close proximity and gotten to know one another as well if 9/11 and the events that followed had not occurred. My agents even comforted a number of my friends' broken hearts—who better to ask for male relationship advice than the two guys sitting in the front seat of the car with you?

I traveled often, even in college, and particularly after graduating, when I lived in South Africa and worked in a children's hospital. On long layovers for transatlantic flights, Steve and I played Scrabble or just talked. During one long flight, I asked him why he had joined the Secret Service. He didn't look like the stereotypical secret agent. If you were casting a movie, Steve probably wouldn't get a callback. The first impression he gave was of someone kind and earnest, rather than muscular and macho.

He became interested in the Secret Service when Ronald Reagan was shot in 1981. Steve had gone to college at the University of Maryland and studied psychology, and each year, the students spent time in a different psych ward. In his third year, he went once a week to a hospital that housed the criminally insane. He spent his time with one man there: John Hinckley Jr., the man who had shot Ronald Reagan. They watched television together and Steve met John's girlfriend, who was another patient. Steve decided that he wanted to protect future presidents and their families from men like Hinckley and others who were determined to do them harm.

After Steve, Scott was appointed as my detail lead and accompanied me on many overseas trips during my dad's second term. Inevitably, when we were traveling together, people would ask how we knew each other. If Scott or any of my agents answered truthfully, it would immediately expose us. Therefore, Scott became fictitious family when he would reply, without even thinking about it, that he was my brother. Finally, I had a brother! Forget that we looked nothing alike, and the age difference was substantial, but people nodded and accepted our fiction. We looked like one big, happy, disproportionately male-dominated family.

And like any family we had our awkward moments. When I was in college, several of my dorm mates convinced me to go to a World Wrestling Federation event at Madison Square Garden. (I'm still not quite sure why I said yes.) The Secret Service was following behind us when we went through a tollbooth. The driver of my car had an E-ZPass, but for some reason my agents didn't; their vehicle hadn't been issued one. They were stuck in the Cash Only lane. It was dark. I sailed down the road, having no idea that they had lost us and were far behind. Only when I got back to my room did I learn what had happened; and, not long after that, stories of my "ditching" my agents made the press. But by far the biggest and most public debacle with my agents occurred during a trip that Jenna and I took together. When I was twenty-five, I went to visit Jenna, who was living in Latin America with some friends, for our birthday. We arrived in Buenos Aires and went straight to a restaurant in San Telmo, the city's main square. It is one of the most touristy areas, but we were excited to catch the Sunday market and have a leisurely wine-filled lunch.

I put my purse under the table, felt it with my foot, and then suddenly it was gone. Someone had reached under and stolen it. The couple next to us had their suitcases and passports stolen too. They were crying and I was shocked. My wallet and cell phone were in my bag, and my agents started calling my phone, hoping the thief might be persuaded to give it back. A man's voice answered once and hung up. He never picked it up again. Suddenly an incident that happens hundreds of times in crowded cities became international news—because someone was now in possession of the numbers on my flip phone, and a genuine "bad guy" had been able to get close enough to touch me.

Commentators began questioning the Secret Service. That made me angry—angry that they were unjustly criticizing their competence. They had followed us to a spot we chose—a touristy destination—and now they were being blamed by a judgmental media and even their bosses. Protection did not absolve us from commonplace happenings, yet being in the limelight suggested it should have. For three long days, the story refused to die. I had become familiar with the harsh ways of the press, and I had blocked it out. Finally, my mom intervened and reminded everyone that the agents' job was not to watch my purse, but to watch me. I could always buy another purse.

Sadly, that lunch was the last incognito moment Jenna and I spent in Buenos Aires. From then on, we were met with shutter-clicking paparazzi. In the United States, aside from our embarrassing party pics, photographers largely left us alone. We didn't sell magazines or provide clickbait online.

In Argentina, it was different. The theft was news. We checked into our hotel, and when we came down to see the city, the lobby had the feel of a Hollywood red carpet. There were live news trucks, with their exoskeletal satellite dish antennas; and a throng of photographers, their shutters rapidly clicking and chronicling our every move. Occasionally, a blinding flash would hit our confused eyes. We changed hotels and the paparazzi followed; it was the hotels who were phoning, giving away our location on what must have been a slow Argentine news day.

Even worse, when we arrived in Argentina, no one knew what we looked like, but now with our photos splashed on the front pages of newspapers, everyone did. People were actively looking for us. It was as if we had suddenly been transformed into Princess Diana or Paris Hilton. We gave up on hotels and retreated to an apartment belonging to family friends of one of our Secret Service agents, unable to go anywhere, unable to fall in love with Argentina. As we stayed holed up, it felt as if Buenos Aires had made us an attraction rather than the other way around.

Federal law mandated that Jenna and I have Secret Service protection for a few months after our dad left office. At the end, a female agent named Genie was in charge of my detail. Her parents were Greek and she spoke Greek, Italian, French, Spanish, Arabic, and English, and she was also very motherly. For eight years I had bypassed the worst of airport security—with at least one armed agent, we always went through a separate security line. Because of that, I hadn't ever had to pay attention to the hassle of the three-ounce liquid plastic container rule—it didn't apply to us.

For my first "solo" flight, which coincidentally was my last day with protection, I was flying to Malawi. I was packed and ready to go, armed with the confidence that I could do this without my unique posse, but Genie was waiting outside my apartment. In the sweetest gesture, and on her off-duty day, she insisted on showing up in her own car to drive me to the airport. On the way, she gave me a pep talk about how I was going to be "great" when I went through security, probably silently wondering if I'd be pulled aside for the name on my driver's license. The Holly Crawford alias had been put to rest, and now I was back to the challenges of being named Barbara Bush. When I did finally turn around and see no one behind me, it was an odd, unexpected feeling: an overwhelming sense of being free.

Now I travel around the world by myself often (and I know all the TSA rules and regulations, along with the specificities of the Southwest boarding process). But no matter how far I travel, hindsight wields its magic power and I think back on that last day, that expression of "I just want to take care of you one last time," and the images return of all those years when someone truly did watch over me, my United States Secret Service angels.

Two Sisters Walk into a Mexican Restaurant...

JENNA

The first time Barbara and I got into trouble, really big trouble, we were three and a half and at our grandparents' house in Maine. We had been kissed good night and safely tucked into bed before sunset. But we knew that everyone else was still up, the grown-ups at dinner, the older kids talking, reading, or watching TV. Lying there, watching the dimming light seep in through the edges of the curtains, we conspired to get up right at that moment and tiptoe outside to the yard to play. Down the stairs and out a side screen door, we raced in our billowing nightgowns and bare feet over to the seawall high above the rocks that led to the ocean.

And that's exactly where the Secret Service, patrolling the grounds of the vice president's summer home, found us, sandy and a bit damp from the ocean's spray. They hoisted us up into their arms and carried us into the house, straight into the dining room, where they announced, "Look who we found on the seawall." The adults were shocked, our parents horrified, thinking about what might have happened to us had we fallen the ten feet to the rocks below. But more than their stern words telling us, "Never do this again," what chastened us was the awful sense that we had deeply disappointed our mom and dad. We cried in unison, and we never did do it again, never snuck out of our rooms to play by the rocks and stare at the sea.

We were hardly the first Bush children to fall short of the mark and receive a parental reprimand. My dad tells the story of the time that he drove home a bit inebriated and plowed into a neighbor's trash can. Ganny saw and heard the whole thing. When he walked in the door, she told him, "Your behavior is disgraceful," and sent him upstairs to see his father. Dad walked in, defiant, and Gampy, who had been reading, took off his glasses, stared hard at my dad, and then put his glasses back on and returned to reading. The knowledge that he had disappointed his own father stung so deeply that there was nothing left to say. That devastated my dad more than any harsh words could have.

My parents, both of whom had grown up in homes with unconditional love and high expectations, opted to raise us in much the same way. There are many modern theories of parenting, but George and Laura Bush didn't see a great need to deviate from what had worked to raise them. We were expected to be good people, to care about others, and to be responsible. Not unlike with Gampy, all it takes from my mother is a single look to know when you have fallen short.

But Barbara and I are also our dad's daughters. For years, we tried to walk right up to that line. And sometimes we truly discovered its location only after having crossed it.

As teenagers, we were serial pranksters, putting emerald food coloring in an unsuspecting houseguest's shampoo, thinking it would dye his hair green. (It did give it a slight greenish tint.) If we saw a prank on TV, we would try it together, or egg the other on to perform solo. Once when we were riding on golf carts at Camp David, at the supposedly mature age of nineteen, I told Barbara to fall off the cart to see what Mom would do. She did, but the only ones we ended up scaring were the Secret Service, who came racing over to her rescue. They were so fast our mom missed the whole thing.

While we were still in high school, we had rules and a curfew—we had to wake up our dad to say good night when we got home. But our lives were not micromanaged; Barbara spent a semester going to school in Rome, completely out of our parents' view. For better or worse, we were free to make our own mistakes, and hopefully to learn from them. And, as everyone knows, *mistakes were made.*

When your parent is inaugurated president, no one from the White House usher's office helpfully steps forward with a manual for presidential children. The role is undefined. When our dad became president, he assured us that we could continue to be normal college kids, saying, "You can do anything that anybody else does." And we took him at his word. (Obviously, he didn't get a manual either!)

Like at most colleges, one of the big things to do at the University of Texas at Austin, where I was a first-year student, was for older girls, who had already turned twenty-one, to give the younger ones their IDs. Of course, the reason why you might want an ID before you were twenty-one was to drink alcohol. Most of my friends had IDs from older girls, and I didn't think anything about it. When you're a college student, you are more preoccupied with who's having a party or who's playing beer pong than if your fake ID will land you in the tabloids. I never stopped to consider, "Oh, wait a minute, now that my dad is president, people are going to recognize me." I just wanted to be like my friends, and I was—although when I went wild, I ended up on a double-page spread in the *National Enquirer*, with a huge caption reading "Pals say she's a hard-drinking party animal." The headline: "Get Ready America, Here Comes George W.'s Wild Daughter." Now, as a thirty-something mom of two daughters, a mom whose clothes are usually sticky from someone's leftover juice box, I almost can't believe that there were ever photos of me in mid-fall next to one of my girlfriends, both of us holding cigarettes. About the only thing I'm grateful for is that I had the foresight to choose a big cross-body bag, which blocked a full-on view of my twisted skirt.

There were two constants in the articles that popped up throughout the spring of 2001: I was always accompanied by an "unidentified friend." When I was charged with an MIP (minor in possession), CNN, the *Washington Post*, and the *New York Times* all noted that, according to the police, Bush and the unidentified friend "were not arrested." (Today, my "unidentified friend" would probably be a meme on Twitter and Instagram.) The last line of every story was invariably: "Her twin sister, Barbara, attends Yale University."

The apparently previously innocent Yalie was publicly corrupted in May. After school and exams were over, Barbara and I went out to dinner with a high school friend at Chuy's, a Mexican restaurant in Austin. Everyone was ordering margaritas. So Barbara and I did, too, and I helpfully pulled out my adult ID. *Yes, I was actually that naive.* Knowing me back then, I had probably requested the table for Jenna Bush, party of three. Even Barbara, the Ivy Leaguer in our group, didn't stop to consider how much more recognizable we were as our twin selves, two together rather than one. Of course, the restaurant's manager dialed 911. In the police report, the officer who arrived quoted the manager as saying, "I want to get them in big trouble." (For anyone wondering why the Secret Service didn't intervene right away, managing teenage antics is not their job. They weren't there to be our babysitters, just to make sure we didn't end up in any unduly dangerous situations. Tex-Mex food, even with a somewhat hostile manager, wouldn't qualify. They were sitting outside in a parked car while we went in.)

Barbara and I did get magazine cover stories and a forever line in our respective Wikipedia entries, but the thing I dreaded most didn't happen.

I called my dad that night, waking him up. I felt that same crushing disappointment I had felt as a three-and-a-half-year-old in Maine. As I began saying how sorry I was, he interrupted and said, "No, I'm sorry. We promised you normalcy, and this is not normal." My parents did make it clear that they weren't thrilled with our behavior, but I'm sure they also recognized that another type of punishment was about to descend. Barbara's and my faces were suddenly everywhere, and the words accompanying them were almost universally negative.

There's probably no greater humiliation for a couple of nineteen-year-old girls than to land on the cover of *People* magazine in a badly angled inauguration photo, where we looked particularly round-faced, with the headline "The

Bush Girls' Latest Scrape: Oops, They Did It Again." *People* was the magazine I read in every checkout line, and I don't think I bought anything for a week to avoid seeing my face when I went up to the counter to pay. I personally preferred the cover of the *New York Post*, which used a much better photo (thank you very much) and dubbed me the pithy "Jenna and Tonic."

Even the outfit I wore to court in Austin to plead no contest was scrutinized via a telephoto lens. The breathless reporting stated: "For her court appearance, she wore a black tank top, pink capri pants, sandals, and a toe ring." (Note to younger readers: Toe rings aren't the best courtroom accessory!) My supposed "tank top" was in fact a sweater borrowed from my roommate. Still, I'd like to tell my nineteen-year-old self to get herself to a mall and buy a dress.

But despite how awkward it was and how miserable it often felt to be overwhelmed with so much unwanted attention, Barbara and I were given a gift by our parents: There were no press secretaries and public relations agents spinning our stories. No stylists hovering over us, presenting us with what to wear, or media consultants coaching us on what to say. For those couple of weeks, we were the scandal du jour, and no real-life Olivia Pope was dispatched to make it all go away. But we learned that we could be imperfect and our lives would go on. I hope that if anyone ever does write a rule book for presidential children, they'll make that the first line.

Every day with my girls, Mila and Poppy, I am silently thankful to my parents for teaching me how to be a parent without the pressure of having to create perfect kids. And also to their own parents, who taught them that lesson first.

E-mail to my granddaughters Jenna, Barbara and Lauren

Subject: Nervous grandfather

March 9, 2003

It is Sunday morning. I am at my duty station in the office. I am worrying about three of my older granddaughters. Spring Break causes the worry. I wonder—are all three off somewhere trying to get on the Wild College Women TV show? Are they having a good time? Are they sticking near their three campuses so they can do what, well, what I used to do during spring break back in the good old days, circa 1946-47-48. Namely, stick near the Library. I found it was almost free of noise and people during spring break. Maybe you three have discovered the same thing. I am here all week in Houston in case you need adult leadership. In spite of these worries, maybe because of these worries, I love all three of you "guys" (who says the Gampster can't be "with it"?)

Devotedly,
Gampy

Celebrity Sightings

JENNA

Let's be clear: Hollywood and Republicans don't always mix, but that didn't mean Barbara and I didn't have hope. Not that it wasn't fun to hang out with the Oak Ridge Boys, but as teenagers we wished that maybe just once Justin Timberlake would make a surprise visit to the White House.

Up until that point, our biggest celebrity encounter was when we watched Linda Ronstadt sing at Gampy's first inauguration (we couldn't take our eyes off her awesomely long hair), and, later that afternoon, we met Shirley Temple when she stood in front of us in line for the bathroom. I was thrilled when she offered me a stick of Trident. By age seven, Barbara and I had watched some of her movies, and a Shirley Temple was our favorite drink. But we couldn't quite process that the blond, giggly Shirley Temple we knew from film was now a tall, dark-haired woman. I did have the presence of mind to ask her for her autograph.

My dad's own inauguration featured Beyoncé, except that she was nineteen, the same age as us, and not quite Queen Bey yet. She was one of three singers in Destiny's Child, a musical group from Texas. Before she took the stage, she gave Barbara and me three-way pagers, where you could send messages to a group. Then Beyoncé spoke to us the magical words "Please keep in touch." Unfortunately, neither Barbara nor I could figure out how to work the pagers. But I've since wondered, if we found them again, could I page Beyoncé and set up a playdate for Mila and Blue Ivy?

I did get a private message once from Katie Holmes. I was a huge fan of hers on *Dawson's Creek*—my friends and I used to watch the series almost every week. And as I was watching her on television during the show's final season, she left me a message on my old Nokia flip phone. She wanted to come and shadow me to prepare for her role in *First Daughter*, a movie where the president's daughter falls in love with her Secret Service agent, who is pretending to be her college residential adviser. Katie was playing the first daughter. (For the record, the original concept for the movie was developed in 1999, when Chelsea Clinton was the official first daughter. And although some of my agents were really handsome, I never fell in love with them. I'm also quite sure that none of them ever fell for me; I was twenty and my photos made regular appearances in the *National Enquirer*. But one of my friends did kiss a particularly handsome agent after we graduated college. And my mom's personal assistant in the White House, Lindsey, fell in love with and married a Secret Service agent.)

I was so struck to have a message from *Katie Holmes*. And then I thought about Katie accompanying me to class, studying with me for my psychology exam, or being my wingman at

Our parents loved that they each had a baby to hold—even before she could say anything, Jenna was preparing to perform.

Our mom wrote of this photo, "Barbara and Jenna were the answer to our prayers."

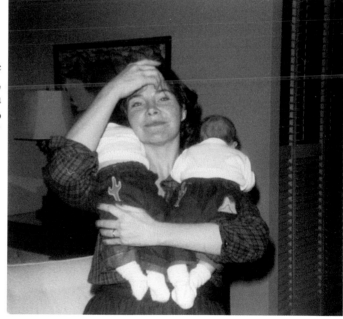

Showing some leg to Reagan-Bush supporters in Midland Texas, 1984. *George Bush Presidential Library and Museum*

Rallying all vampires and gum chewers to vote for our Gampy on Halloween in 1988. *George Bush Presidential Library and Museum*

Holding tight to the newly elected president. #firstblowout *George Bush Presidential Library and Museum*

With our much-loved Pa and Grammee in Midland, Texas.

Double Trouble from Day
Our personalities didn't
but our outfits sure did.

George Bush Presidential Library and Museum

Baseball was our family sport—we adored the Texas Rangers players so much that we named our dog Spot Fetcher after shortstop Scott Fletcher. *Courtesy of the Texas Rangers*

Knee socks and lots of rocks: family photo at Walker's Point with Gampy, Uncle Jeb, George P., Noelle, and Jebby Jr. *George Bush Presidential Library and Museum*

On the water in
Kennebunkport,
where our
grandfather is
most at peace. We
look pretty happy
too. *George Bush
Presidential Library
and Museum*

Fine dining at
the White House
while Gampy was
president, circa
1990. *George Bush
Presidential Library
and Museum*

Original *Mario Brothers*, baby! Camp David, 1990. *George Bush Presidential Library and Museum*

Gampy, dressed to wage "cold war," throwing snow at Camp David. *George Bush Presidential Library and Museum*

Reading *Santa and Friends* on the night before Christmas. We went to Camp David every year our grandfather was president. *George Bush Presidential Library and Museum*

Five little grandchildren under the tree. While Barbara watched the cousins, Jenna checked out the swag. *George Bush Presidential Library and Museum*

Christmas circa 1992, or as we call it, the year of the #epicfashionfail #tie. *George Bush Presidential Library and Museum*

Barbara and her beautiful Swedish roommate, Josefine, in Italy in 1998.

Dad, Jenna, Mom, and Barbara's left ear at the 2001 inauguration. *Courtesy of the George W. Bush Presidential Library and Museum*

Father-daughter inaugural balling in 2001. *Courtesy of the George W. Bush Presidential Library and Museum*

On board *Air Force One. Courtesy of the George W. Bush Presidential Library and Museum*

Family portrait, inauguration morning 2001. *Courtesy of the George W. Bush Presidential Library and Museum*

Blushing with words of *amore* with former Italian prime minister Silvio Berlusconi. *Courtesy of the George W. Bush Presidential Library and Museum*

With our namesakes, Jenna Welch and Barbara Bush, at Camp David in 2003. *Courtesy of the George W. Bush Presidential Library and Museum*

Getting wild at the White House holiday parties in 2004. *Courtesy of the George W. Bush Presidential Library and Museum*

Barbara, the "little mascot" of the 2008 US men's Olympic basketball team in Beijing—and yes, that is LeBron James. *Courtesy of the George W. Bush Presidential Library and Museum*

ur mom giving a toast at Jenna's rehearsal dinner. *Paul Morse Photography*

Henry joins our sisters' "beasthood" on Jenna's wedding day at the fishing pond on the ranch at Crawford. *Paul Morse Photography*

Jenna and Henry on Cadillac Mountain at sunrise, right after they got engaged in 2007.

Mom and Mila take Manhattan in 2015.

Barbara's Secret Service detail chief, Steve—probably the only USSS agent with a secret Wu-Tang Clan name. *Annie Dickinson*

Jenna with the *Today Show* crew returning to the White House in 2015. *Samantha Okazaki/TODAY*

Welcoming Poppy Louise into the sisters fold on August 14, 2015.

Global Health Corps alumni selfie in Rwanda, 2017. *Mpindi Abaas*

Sisters first and always.

a party, where everyone would be falling all over themselves because it was Katie Holmes. I knew that my real life was going to be a complete disappointment compared to anything in a Hollywood script. So I never called her back. Fifteen years later, I met Katie Holmes in New York and I had to say, "Remember that message you left me once? I'm so sorry I never returned your call."

The only genuine celebrity "friend" I had when my dad was in office wasn't even mine—he was my dad's. Bono, the lead singer of U2, became close with my dad through their work combatting HIV/AIDS and other health crises in Africa—recently, he helicoptered out to my parents' ranch to have lunch. They have a great friendship, and as a side benefit, I occasionally got some special fan status. The first time I ever used it was when I went to a U2 concert right around the end of college. Gwen Stefani and No Doubt were the opening act, and something about the crowd, the heat, and the strobe lights caused me to faint and crash to the ground. One second I was stepping side to side to the music and the next I was blinking my eyes and wondering why everyone was staring down at me. I woke up, but the Secret Service was worried. I had a backstage pass, so they took me backstage, and I ended up in Bono's dressing room. In the midst of all the music and moving parts, it was completely pristine. There was a white carpet on the floor and an artful display of crystals; everything was very Zen. I sat in Bono's chair, sipping cold water and recovering from my humiliation.

I did go backstage other times and talk to Bono—but my most successful fan moment was probably that time when I sat in his chair, alone, because I didn't have to say anything. All the other times, I would end up telling Bono about whatever U2 song I loved, which was probably the most boring conversation he'd had all evening. Fortunately, he always found a charming way to change to a more interesting subject.

By far, though, the best celebrity encounter either of us ever had belonged to Barbara. She met LeBron James at the Beijing Olympics, and after some joking around, he passed along his number. Henry and I had visions of a Bush–James basketball dynasty. We could see ourselves living comfortably in their guesthouse...But just like Justin Timberlake unplugged at the White House, it was not to be. Or, to quote U2, "I still haven't found what I'm looking for."

9/11

BARBARA

I went to college far away from Texas, on the East Coast, at Yale University. My dad had gone to Yale as well, but that particular tie was ephemeral at best. We weren't one of those families who made nostalgic pilgrimages back for college class reunions or drank out of college seal coffee mugs. I was drawn to New Haven because of its proximity to glamorous New York, intrigued by the many Yale professors whose published books were on my parents' bookshelf.

The campus itself looks like Hogwarts, intertwined with a mini-city, an industrial port whose heyday was in the 1950s. Urban buildings surround the soaring Gothic and Georgian buildings. Yale itself resembles a quilt of small New England town squares with grassy greens for lounging and congregating, guarded by towering locked wrought-iron gates upon which perch blue strobe panic lights. The contrast between the city and the university is sobering.

My sophomore year, I lived in Davenport College, in a dorm room with three other girls, all sharing two adjoining bedrooms.

On September 10, my roommate Laura and I fell asleep talking about her then crush (and now husband). Our radio alarm woke us up every morning to the daily newscast. As it went off, and we opened our eyes to bright sunshine, we heard something surprising: A plane had struck one of the Twin Towers in Manhattan. The radio announcer reported it as an accident. My cell phone rang. Steve, my Secret Service man, was on the other end. Everything was about to change.

Although I was too young to remember, I first met Steve when my grandfather was elected president. Steve had been assigned to protect our immediate family. Then the threat had been from Central and South American drug cartels. The cartels were fixated on my grandfather and his bloodlines, so my dad, as the president's son, had an agent assigned to protect him, and Jenna and I, as the president's granddaughters, had them as well. That was twelve years before 9/11, when Steve was a twenty-five-year-old agent who rotated through our Texas home.

In late 2000, Steve received a call while serving on President Clinton's detail. The Secret Service wanted to know if he was interested in overseeing my detail. He was told that seven other agents had put in their names. His response was "Sure, add mine." The next day, he received a second call, telling him he had gotten the job. "What?" he remembers asking. "No interview? What about the seven other guys?" The voice at the other end was confused. "What seven other people? You were the only one who volunteered." It's safe to say his assignment was not all that coveted. Before Steve left to meet me in Texas, his boss sat him down and told him bluntly that he was being "set up to fail." As he put it, you'll be following around a feisty eighteen-year-old girl who doesn't want security. I had made that sentiment clear when I met with Steve's boss. I was an extremely private teenager, looking forward to the freedom of college.

Steve tried harder than I did at the start. He made sure "his guys" stayed way in the background. They always respectfully stayed out of my dorm. Everyone on the detail was young, in their early twenties and thirties and dressed like college kids, except that in their backpacks, rather than books and a CD or MP3 player, they were packing heat. I'm grateful for the extreme lengths they went to to blend in— it wasn't easy. "Spot the Agent" became a game to other kids on campus. I'd notice unknown students would look at me, maybe take a second look, and then immediately start searching, trying to figure out who my Secret Service guys were. Sometimes they would walk up to an agent, saying, "Hey, I know who you are," letting the agents know they couldn't be fooled, that this student was in on the secret too. But other times, they would mistakenly call out a football player or another athlete who happened to be crossing the quad at the same time. Turns out "Spot the Agent" wasn't so easy. Steve was once devastated when I cut through a little campus convenience store, Durfee's, and as he followed me, he held the door for another student. She looked at him and said, "Thanks, sir." He was crushed. It was a reminder that though he was trying his best to blend in as just another college kid, he was closing in on thirty-seven.

On a trip to New Orleans with my best friend Matthew, we convinced Steve to join us in taking an online quiz—

a forerunner to the endless BuzzFeed quizzes that tell you which *90210* character you'd be or which animal is your spirit animal—to reveal his Wu-Tang Clan name. If Steve had been in Wu-Tang, he would have been dubbed "Bastard Bastard Harbor Master." I found this hilarious—proper Steve as "Bastard Bastard Harbor Master"—and teased him about it relentlessly.

I grew to respect and like Steve, but I could never forget why he was there, or why I had his number programmed into the speed dial on my phone. Whenever he called, I was worried.

Steve knew we didn't have a television in our room, so his call was just a simple heads-up, a "Hey, I just want to let you know—if you're not listening to the radio, the second Twin Tower has been hit in New York and it's unclear what's happened, so we need to be on you more today." This was shocking—how could two planes have accidentally hit the Twin Towers?

Around 9:30, as I was gathering my books to rush out for class, somebody knocked and asked for me. Emily, one of my roommates, thought it was a random classmate. I heard a guy's voice, and Emily asking, "How do you know Barbara?" She was protecting me, pretending I had already gone for the morning. I hung back, uncertain, as he kept saying, "I need to talk to Barbara," finally adding, "Tell her I'm with Steve the Bastard." It was a code. Emily stepped aside once she heard the name, and I rushed out of the room. Tony, the agent, said, "You've got to come with me, and we've got to get out of here right now." I knew then that something far worse had happened with those planes, but exactly what, I was unsure. I was nervous and scared but comforted by Tony's presence, by his plan. We raced down the stairs and away from the elegant brick facade of Davenport College, across the stone walkways and the grassy green, to a waiting SUV, the engine running. I took nothing, not my backpack, not my contacts, I didn't even take a jacket as the day had started out so beautiful, all blue sky.

We didn't go far, just to the Secret Service office in downtown New Haven. It was a completely sterile office with what looked like rented furniture. Nothing on the tables, nothing on the walls, nothing to look at except a window or the television. So we turned on the television.

Many members of my detail were based out of the Secret Service's New York field office, and those offices were in— of all places—7 World Trade Center. It was not one of the Twin Towers, but a separate building in the complex. When the North Tower collapsed, flaming debris hit Tower 7. All morning, we watched the footage. And all morning I cried. For them, this was where they went to work when they were not with me; this was the city where their families lived. This was home. Their job at that moment was to protect me. But I could hear them each whispering into their phones, calling their families, calling their colleagues and friends. Their usually stoic, emotionless faces were ashen. Because my own parents were rushed to secure locations—my mother in a safe building in DC, my father circling in the air above the United States aboard *Air Force One*—I had no direct number to use to reach them.

We were all scared and alone together, and I look back now and realize that we became a family that afternoon.

The Secret Service put Jenna and me in touch. I wonder now if they knew the only true way they could comfort me was to dial my sister. Maybe they saw the longing on my face when they spoke to their loved ones. It was a relief to hear her voice, but I was anxious to talk to my mom and my dad.

My mother did call later that morning from her secure location. She was calm, the way she always is, and was calling to check on me and assure me she was safe. She told me to turn off the television, but it was too hypnotic. The only thing worse than watching was the unknown of not watching.

The afternoon wore on and the streets turned silent; the pedestrians had gone home. The skies were empty, every plane grounded. The enveloping silence outside seemed to make the TV even louder and the office windows more exposed. The Secret Service knew that for safety reasons—with so many unknown potential threats—we needed to find a place where no one could easily find us. That meant a hotel where we could pay cash, making us untraceable. There were plenty of hotels in New Haven, but those would be too obvious. We piled into the Expedition and headed for a Holiday Inn off the highway in North Haven. It was a squat brown building with balcony walkways and an exposed parking lot in front. The perfect stopping-off point for truckers or tourists or lovers, for whom $59 a night seemed like a bargain. The perfect place to take cover.

I was there when my dad called. I was scared and needed him. Despite the Secret Service suggesting he and my mom sleep in a bunker for the night, he calmly shared that they would be sleeping together at the White House; that normality, or as close to normality as possible, was necessary. While that, of course, seemed risky to me, I knew he was right. He let me know he was okay, but he, like our nation, was hurting. I could hear the pain in his voice, but also the resiliency. He had a job to do, a country to attend to, so the call was short.

He hung up with his usual "I love you, baby," an ending that is indelibly written on my heart. Minutes later, he walked up to the podium to address the nation.

We watched as much of his speech as we could, but the hotel TV reception was grainy and fading in and out. The Holiday Inn was even lonelier and emptier than the office building. Not another soul was staying there. Our meals were from vending machines—chips and candy and orange-cheese-filled crackers. The rooms smelled unused, two double beds with slippery bedspreads, a scratchy carpet, a wood veneer chest, a telephone book, and a television. We tried to hunt down books or magazines in the lobby for a respite from repeated images of the Twin Towers on TV. Steve's wife and five-year-old daughter drove up from New York to stay with him—he wanted them out of the city—and his daughter jumped on the bed with abandon, overjoyed to have a hotel slumber party with her parents. It was so stark, the juxtaposition of her joy with every image flickering on the television screen.

I spent the next day largely by myself in my room. I had always loved solitude and being alone with my thoughts. But now the hours dragged and my mind wandered. I was scared—scared of the unknown, scared of what the attack meant for our country, for the world. I wondered if my parents were safe and if they would remain so. That night, my agents brought my roommates to join me—an incredibly sweet gesture. When they arrived, I was embarrassed that one of my roommates saw an earnest note I had written on the hotel pad and placed by my bed—"The sun still rises"—inspired by my shock upon waking to a beautiful day on September 12. The weather did not match the somber, foreboding feeling.

By then the vending machines were empty, so we rallied the agents and headed to Taco Bell in the tinted-window Expedition. It was vaguely exotic because none of us had cars in college, so drive-thru food was a luxury. There was no wait, because there were almost no cars on the road and we were the only ones in the drive-thru lane.

The next day, I went back to school. That weekend, I headed to Camp David to be with my parents, and also, if possible, to distract them, to lighten the burden that had descended upon my dad. I wanted the comfort and safety of my parents. I secretly hoped it would allow us all to feel normal again, like our protected pack. Jenna arrived from Texas and we were briefly our usual foursome once again.

When I returned to campus, the weather was beautiful, the atmosphere grim. Going to school in the Northeast meant many people were from New York—one of my roommates was a Manhattan-bred New Yorker who used to pat me on the head, amused by my Texas "quaintness" when I asked questions. So many of them knew family members or a friend's father or mother who had been in the Towers that morning. There was nervousness and fear and a sense of hunkering down. Everyone was shocked and sad. It was sunny in New Haven, but it was quiet, silent at the core, as if there were no breeze or birdsong.

Yale, like the United States, eventually returned to the new normal. The sophomores hurrying to class across the Davenport quad today are about the same age as Steve's daughter is now, his daughter who once jumped on the motel bed with the pure joy of a five-year-old. I will never forget the sounds of those days and the following weeks and months, the sterile rooms and the terrible quiet, when everything changed.

First Pitch

BARBARA

Baseball has always been our family sport. Though Jenna and I were pathetic, dare I say shitty, players, we spent hours practicing with a yellow plastic bat while our dad threw slow pitches in the front yard. In our team softball games, we'd play our positions, but I preferred to get lost in left field— making rings out of long grass stems or practicing dance moves until a ball bounced in my direction. I'd panic at both my delayed reaction and the distance I had to throw, while my parents watched, elbowing each other, laughing.

Before politics, professional baseball was front and center in our lives. We went to baseball games the way other families sat down to a nightly dinner. We had four seats in a row, and when the Texas Rangers were in town, we would be in the stadium. Our dad was one of the owners, but more than that, he loved (and still loves) to sit beside our mom and watch the game. Jenna and I, however, could stand to sit in our assigned seats only for the first few pitches and then we would take off, winding our way through the concourse and the stands— a huge playground for almost nine innings. We stopped to have our baseball cards made. We almost always got ice cream scoops in miniature baseball hats—exotic flavors like white chocolate macadamia nut—or when it was deep into summer, the delicious frozen lemon chill. At home we watched very little television, since it was off-limits on school nights, so one of our favorite things to do was to sneak into the owner's box and turn on the TV. We'd watch scandalous Lifetime movies like *Love, Lies and Murder,* which we'd never be allowed to watch at home. We got away with it, too, until the seventh-inning stretch, when my mom would stand up and turn around to look for us. She would invariably see Jenna and me, dancing the do-si-do together to whatever country song was playing over the loudspeaker in the stadium. She would also see the TV glowing in the background. If we caught her eyes, she would shake her head and mouth "off," and we would sheepishly find the remote and head back down to our designated row.

While my friends were into boy bands or teen heartthrob actors, Jenna and I were obsessed with baseball players. When we walked through the underground of the stadium with my dad, we would peek around a corner or pause outside the locker-room door, hoping for a glimpse of the catcher, the outfielders, the shortstop, or the second baseman. To us, they looked like movie stars. Jenna's favorite was Rubén Sierra and mine was Julio Franco. We would go crazy whenever they were at bat. We would cheer and cheer, "Go, Rubén!"; "Go, Julio!" until we were hoarse. I still remember Julio Franco's wedding; he wore a gold tux and kissed us each on the cheek.

I considered it my first real kiss; the fact that he was marrying another woman meant nothing.

We knew all the players down the roster: their names, some of their stats, and what position they played. Every spring break, we traveled to Rangers spring training in Florida, where the tropical sun turned our arms and shoulders a heated pink. We watched almost all the games and memorized the new players' names. (Baseball was so baked into our family culture that our first password for our family online accounts, Prodigy and then AOL, was "Ranger," which each of us could easily remember.)

My dad loved baseball, but the rest of us loved something more than the sport. It was the rhythmic slowness of the game, the rituals, and the shimmering dome of Texas heat that slowed time to a crawl from the moment we took our seats. Win or lose, my dad was always relaxed, taking it all in. People often came up to him when we sat in the stands. Each season, the line of people asking him for his autograph grew longer, and increasingly they would ask, "Are you going to run?" It became so common that I stopped paying attention, and after a while it seemed like any other question: "How's the team going to do this season?"; "Do you think they can beat the Angels?"; "Will the rain hold off?" But looking back, that question planted the seed that our easy nights were going to change.

We went to the games occasionally after my dad was elected governor and we had moved to Austin, but it was different. My dad had to travel with security, and even though we could still have the run of the stadium, we were older. We were no longer thrilled by peanuts and chili dogs and stadium snacks or awed with finding nooks and crannies beside the stairwells. No longer regulars, we discovered that many of the people we knew had also moved on.

In college, I didn't pay attention to baseball. Except for one game, the only one I ever attended with my parents while my dad was president. It was played in New York City in the fall of 2001.

When you are in college, you don't see your parents much. Jenna and I had both gone home to be with our dad and mom on the weekend after 9/11, but I hadn't seen them since. Then on October 30, my dad was invited to throw out the first pitch at game three of the World Series, which featured the New York Yankees versus the Arizona Diamondbacks. Jenna was in school in Austin, but Yankee Stadium was a short ride from Yale, so I decided to go.

I brought a couple of friends who I knew liked baseball. One, Teddy Pataki, was the son of the governor of New York, George Pataki. It was a Tuesday, and Teddy had football practice. We waited and waited with my Secret Service agents outside Yale's football stadium, but Teddy had to run more laps for his coach, so we left without him.

The drive down was quiet, or at least I was. I was worried about what might happen in New York, about what might happen at an event with so many people gathered together, and about what could happen when my dad walked out in front of everyone. In one corner of my mind, I assumed the worst, although I didn't really know what the worst was. As the buildings and billboards came into view, that fear became palpable; I could touch it, just as I could touch the solid, dark glass on the SUV's window. I tried to play it cool, but I was nervous, nervous to the point of tears.

We almost missed the start of the game. Even though I was with Secret Service, the other Secret Service were triple-checking our IDs and holding us back out of caution. Finally, we made it up to the owner's box, which was packed with Secret Service agents. Otherwise, it was a sea of famous New Yorkers—Billy Crystal, Regis Philbin, baseball legend Whitey Ford, and Donald Trump. George Steinbrenner was not pleased that I'd brought two college friends along, taking up more space in an already-crowded room. All around me, people were talking, but in that slightly elevated way most do when they are nervous underneath. For a long time after 9/11, whenever there was a large gathering in New York City, people probably had a nervous feeling in the pit of their stomachs or the back of their minds, the *What if...?* I saw my mom across the box and made a beeline in her direction.

I didn't feel like mingling, and I could tell Mom felt the same way. We huddled together off to one side of the box to protect each other from making small talk about the thing we did not want to mention: my dad warming up beneath the stadium and then waiting in the dugout to walk out, by himself, onto the open field, exposed in front of everyone. The only thing my mom could bring herself to say was "How was the drive down?"

We heard Yankee announcer Bob Sheppard's voice: "Ladies and Gentlemen, the President of the United States." Dad walked out of the Yankees' dugout to the pitcher's mound. Earlier, he said he wasn't sure if he would be able to throw a decent pitch because he'd be wearing a bulletproof vest underneath his New York Fire Department jacket. The vest was constricting and made it hard to throw a strike, let alone a strike from the pitcher's mound. But the Secret Service had insisted he wear it. My dad wanted to throw a perfect pitch because of all that moment symbolized, and he wanted to throw it from the toughest spot on the field: the top of the mound.

The stadium was alive; the floor shook beneath us as tens of thousands of people chanted, "USA! USA!" With every decibel, the pit in my stomach grew. I wanted to turn my eyes away, but I stayed focused on the mound. My dad was there; he rotated around, gave a thumbs-up. And then he pulled back his arm and threw a pitch, a perfect pitch. It sailed fast and true right across home plate and into the catcher's mitt, a strike.

With the pitch, I exhaled all the breath I had been holding and started to cry. These days, I cry all the time at anything moving, but back then, as a sophomore in college, I didn't want to cry, I wanted to be cool.

For all of us—for my mom, for me, for everyone who felt vulnerable that evening—that one pitch was so much more than just a ball uncorking and spinning through the air.

It was also a profound moment for me as a daughter. I was watching my dad step up and do what he needed to do to comfort others. That's what he had always done for me as my father; I knew that about him. I depended on it. But in this moment, that's what he did for everyone. They could feel some of what I had always known.

My dad came up to the box afterward. He had taken off the bulletproof vest. He went directly to my mom and they hugged and kissed. My parents are not affectionate in public; it might have been the only time I've ever seen them kiss in front of others, so I knew that they had both been nervous, both needed comfort. Just knowing that they had been anxious, too, was deeply consoling to me.

My dad watched some pitches and at-bats—this was the first World Series game that he had ever attended—until he left after the third inning.

But for that brief time, those three innings, baseball brought us together again.

Reflections on War

JENNA

When my grandfather went to war against Saddam Hussein after the invasion of Kuwait, he wrote a heartfelt letter to my dad about his worries and his fears. I remember the yellow ribbons tied around the trees throughout our suburban Texas neighborhood, and my dad remembers the gravity of the words his father penned: "I guess what I want you to know as a father is this: Every Human life is precious. When the question is asked 'How many lives are you willing to sacrifice'—it tears at my heart. The answer, of course, is none—none at all."

When my dad was weighing whether to go to war against Iraq, when intelligence reports were telling him that Iraq had chemical weapons and when Saddam Hussein refused to allow weapons inspectors into his country, he wrote his own heartfelt letter to Barbara and me: "Yesterday I made the hardest decision a president has to make. I ordered young Americans into combat. It was an emotional moment for me because I fully understand the risks of war. More than once, I have hugged and wept with the loved ones of a soldier lost in combat in Afghanistan." His words spoke of how much he didn't want to go to war, how he had hoped the battle could be averted. We felt the same.

Throughout my father's time in office, we had families and faces to put with the words: Americans in uniform, especially at Camp David. The presidential retreat at Camp David isn't just a retreat, it's a military installation. The people we saw whenever we visited were primarily active-duty members of the Marines or Navy. Many were our age, twenty or twenty-one, youthful and strong, with their lives still ahead of them.

We knew them, we knew their wives and husbands, we knew their children. We sat next to them at church on Sundays inside the camp chapel. On Christmas Eve, we saw them in their uniforms, with baby girls in fancy dresses and boys in cute sweaters balanced on their laps. We watched their older children act out the Christmas pageant, dressed as sheep and wise men. We heard them caroling. And sometimes they told us good-bye as they were being deployed.

I worried about them, worried about them coming home safely to their children. I prayed for them. And when I glanced at them across the pew, there were times when I felt completely inadequate. They risked their lives to keep everyone I love safe.

I remember the night the bombing started in Iraq. I didn't know when the war would start. I was in college and out with friends when I saw the images flash on a television screen. It was a dark, grainy picture with flashes of bright, greenish light. Some of the people were applauding, but I felt sick. I got up and left to go back to my apartment. All I could think of were the faces of those men and women at Camp David and of the many other service members we had met.

When the war began, Barbara and I were miles away from each other at school. We talked on the phone almost daily—this was before texting took over our communication—and thank goodness, because I wanted to hear Barbara's voice.

It's hard now to remember just how anxious those months and years were after 9/11. In the summer of 2002, I had gone to Camp David for the weekend with my dad and a few of my best friends from Texas. It was early on a Saturday morning and we were still asleep in our cabin when my dad and the Secret Service burst in, waking us up and telling us that there was a plane approaching. In our pajamas, we jumped from our beds and headed down to a network of underground tunnels. There wasn't even time for me to put in my contacts, so I couldn't see. My dad took my hand and led me, as if I were a little girl, through the half darkness down to the area below.

It was a false alarm; a plane had violated the airspace. It was not an attack, but that didn't mean the next time it wouldn't be real. We just never knew for sure.

Throughout my father's years in office, the feelings and emotions were often raw. When Henry went to business school while we were still dating and not yet engaged, we came home more than once to find manila envelopes left by protesters at his door. Each one was filled with threatening notes about how he should be at war, how he should be in combat. He was the only person at the school to get them, and it was only because he was dating me.

I remember when Matt Damon went on TV in 2006 and said that maybe Barbara and I should be sent to Iraq. I had always had a kind of celebrity crush on him; my favorite movie was *Good Will Hunting*. But at that moment, his words stung, in part because I did like him so much, but I also understood the meaning of his words.

There were limits to what Barbara or I could do during those years. After 9/11, the Secret Service restricted where we could travel. There was a Secret Service rule to protect us first, no matter where we were, and even if I was the adult in charge. I know it was for our own protection, but this rule brought its own set of difficulties. In 2007, I took my DC charter school class to visit the Capitol Building. While we were touring, there was a bomb threat. Everyone was ordered to evacuate. My Secret Service detail tried to follow protocol and put me in a secure car. But I insisted that I wouldn't leave my students, that we would all head back to school as a class, together. It was a hard moment for me and for the agents.

One consequence of having come to adulthood in a time of war, a war that began under my father's administration, has been that I will always look at my life and wonder if it is meaningful enough. And I will never forget that the reason I feel safe and free is because the dads and moms of other daughters did not return home.

BARBARA

To write about a war is a difficult task; to write about a war that your dad launched when he was president is almost impossible. I never questioned my dad's intention to do the right thing. But when the subject at hand is war, what is the right thing? Is there even a "right thing"? And however much I might agonize over these questions, it is nothing compared to the agonies felt by my dad.

Once the Iraq War started, there were protesters wherever my dad went on official business. Small clusters would often line the route of his motorcade. Whenever I traveled with him we never looked away, but gazed out the windows, taking in the people and the signs. It was their freedom of speech. One time, as we were traveling down a major street in Washington, I was looking out the window and all of a sudden I spotted a high school friend, Blair. He was standing with the other protesters holding a sign against the war. I wasn't surprised to see him there; although we had never talked politics in high school, I had always known his views. But suddenly, as I saw him, he saw my dad and me. Simultaneously, Blair lowered his sign and started smiling and waving as my dad and I smiled and waved back, mouthing "Hi, Blair." It was exactly like running into an old friend, which is in fact what happened. It is a reminder that in any debate there are humans on all sides.

The war never left my dad. Sometimes I went with him when he visited injured troops at Walter Reed. One Easter we traveled to the large military hospital in San Antonio, Texas. The troops didn't know my dad was coming. We walked in and saw them sitting up in hospital beds surrounded by their families. My dad went from room to room, thanking each one for his or her service and checking on them. It was moving to me, watching them, knowing they were in pain, and yet seeing that they were honored to have my dad visit, while my dad said he was the one who was honored to know them. He was always aware that each of them served because of a decision he had made, and he felt that they were more deserving of his honor than he was of theirs.

I never thought my dad would become an artist. Growing up, I was the artistic one in our family. Family legend says that when I was a toddler, my parents would wake to find me sitting in the living room coloring away. If there was an art class, I registered for it. I particularly loved painting. In high school, I'd paint canvases in my room, and Dad would often walk in to chat. But he was always more interested in our chatting than in the art. So, when my sixty-five-year-old dad mentioned that he'd started painting, I was shocked. His artistic career started with drawings. After he left office and got his first-ever smartphone, he'd text Jenna and me updates of his day, via stick figures drawn on an iPhone app. A stick figure of him waving in a plane window, a stick figure of him riding his bike. He didn't take his "art" too seriously and neither did we.

The next thing I knew, though, he had found an art teacher and purchased oil paints. He painted everything from my cat Eleanor to landscapes in Zambia. When he thought that his skill had matured enough, he turned his brush to people, starting with world leaders he knew well. He created portraits of Great Britain's Tony Blair, Afghanistan's Hamid Karzai, Russia's Vladimir Putin, and the Dalai Lama, among others. His next series of subjects were private figures—people whom he considered to be every bit as consequential: wounded warriors. Just as he had honored heads of state, he wanted to honor these men and women. Typical of my dad, he didn't want to do it in a way that would make him the center of attention. To him, it is the subject that matters most, not the person doing the painting.

Dad was inspired by British prime minister Winston Churchill's book *Painting As a Pastime*, but for my dad, painting has become a passion. My parents have converted the upstairs attic of their Dallas house to an artist's studio, and the first thing Dad asks me whenever I come home is, "Do you want to come up to the studio?" His clothes are now covered in paint (he wears a white lab coat to protect them from further paint splatters, but trust me, there isn't much in his closet that doesn't already have extra colors on it). When he shakes hands, there is invariably paint on his fingertips.

Painting has changed how he views the world. Now, a landscape he's driven past hundreds of times comes to life via a shadow, a color, a tint—he's constantly taking photos of places as inspiration, so he can study the contours and the shading and ultimately capture them in a painting. He notices the world differently, picking out the myriad colors in the sky beyond the traditional "blue." In a similar way, when he stands at his easel, the faces of the wounded warriors he paints also come to life. He works to capture them in all their dimensions.

Recently, I was home in Dallas for a speech, staying with my parents. After dinner one night, with the lights dim throughout the house, I climbed the stairs to my dad's painting studio. Arranged around the walls were hundreds of paintings of men's and women's faces, hundreds of eyes staring back at me. I didn't know these men and women personally, but he did. He had studied each person and could recite their family members' names, their deployment date, their physical and mental wounds, their worries, and ultimately their hopes. He'd studied each wounded warrior both physically, to paint them, and through conversation, to understand them. He does not shy away from listening to and talking about their struggles with PTS (post-traumatic stress—he wants to permanently remove the "D" of "Disorder" from PTSD). He says, "We can't not talk about it. We can't pretend someone is fine when they aren't."

That night, I sat down as a baseball game played on the TV in the background, with a veritable amphitheater of men and women around me, while Dad asked, "Do you want to be my curator?" I did. When we visit, I love talking to him about each painting. I love understanding what or who influences him (he took online courses from the Museum of Modern Art in New York that introduced him to new artists daily). I love seeing his joy in showing off his studio. But I also love the depth of what this art means to him. I see the discipline in his approach and even a type of mindfulness, where he purposely disengages from the electronic world and focuses on the canvas in front of him for hours on end.

To my dad, the meaning is different: His portraits are another way to incorporate people who matter into his life. His wounded-warrior subjects do not simply sit for him; they come to the ranch; they golf and bicycle with him. He shares in their lives, and they share in his. They have become "his people," not only on the canvas, but beyond.

As for me, I still don't know if there will ever be a right answer to any question on war. What I do know is that my dad looked his decision in the face and made it—and in the years since, he has never looked away from the many faces of those it affected. He has always owned his responsibility, personally and deeply, in ways known only to him, ways at which the rest of us, myself included, can only guess.

Dear Barbara and Jenna,

Yesterday I made the hardest decision a President has to make. I ordered young Americans into combat. It was an emotional moment for me because I fully understand the risks of war. More than once I have hugged and wept with the loved ones of a soldier lost in combat in Afghanistan.

I also know my decision will be unpopular on college campuses. I hurt for you because of the pressures on you. There will be marches, loud professors denouncing me and our actions, and bad posters.

I am confident in my decision.

I am also confident that there is an almighty God who will provide comfort, strength, and love. And I pray daily. I pray for those I love. And the three I love the most are you and mom.

Love, DAD

The Dad We Know

BARBARA

In 2004, Jenna and I decided to join our dad's campaign. We had just graduated from college and had a summer free to zigzag across the country in support of our dad. Campaigning is a piecemeal experience—bouncing from rally to town to Holiday Inn and Motel 6, nibbling on trays of white bread sandwiches and pickles on the campaign bus. Jenna and I were the opening act for our mom or our aunt, or, better yet, our dad. Campaigning with Dad was always my favorite, and sometimes, it was just the two of us, alone. One would assume the opposite—because our destination was a stadium full of tens of thousands of people. But the second the heavy black Suburban door closed, it would be just Dad and me, sitting side by side, with time to talk. The stunning thing to me is that while I always thought I knew my dad, where I really got to know *all* of him was not in these private moments, but in very public ones.

For campaign events, I had rehearsed my standard intro

speech over and over—a speech about a dad who drove the car pool in embarrassing hats (do all dads do this?), who without a doubt chose Jenna and me over his career, who embodied love in my eyes. But every time I'd walk up to the podium, I'd become so overwhelmed by the energy and enthusiasm, the yells and claps, of thousands of people cheering for my dad (cheers I never heard while living my East Coast life), I'd have to battle back tears to get through my remarks. As Dad would walk onto the stage, he'd hug me, and the tears would be unleashed. I'd sit on the sidelines, beaming as I listened to him speak, tears streaming down my face. Every now and then, he'd look over at me and wink. And, occasionally, he'd well up too.

Up until that last campaign, I'd shunned political events. I thought they were too scripted and fake, too tedious and boring. I didn't go to events when he was governor of Texas, or rallies during his first presidential campaign. I'd never gotten (and still pretty much don't get) a big boost from being around huge crowds of people. But this was different. For the first time, I saw my dad interact with thousands of complete strangers. I saw how he inspired them, I saw their reactions of appreciation toward him. I saw how emotional they got when he spoke. It was completely different from anything I had experienced—or had expected.

There have been other poignant, private moments that have, ironically enough, come on a public stage. For a long time, my dad has been open about his issues with alcohol. I don't remember when my dad used to drink. I don't remember if he was too loud or boisterous or too willing to make a flippant remark or needle a friend. Jenna and I were four and a half when he stopped. What I knew was that he didn't drink, that when everyone else had a beer at a baseball game, he was the person without a cup in his hand. It was confusing as a child. I didn't grasp the importance of his desire to choose his kids and his family over anything else that might get in the way.

As I became an adult, we talked about it more, about the nuances of knowing when a thing like alcohol is too much to handle, rather than declaring it completely right or completely wrong. But I myself had never heard him speak publicly about alcohol until I went to a speech that he gave for Father's Day 2015. It was the type of speech that I easily could've missed (and I likely have missed many others like it), except that my dad was one of three men receiving "Father of the Year" Awards, and I was presenting him with his statuette. Even so, the topic of his speech sounded saccharine: George W. Bush on his greatest role—dad.

I sat on the dais and I listened as my dad spoke about struggling with alcohol, about how before he became a dad he might have been "slightly self-absorbed at times." And then he said the lines that made me cry: "You see, what happened to me was alcohol was becoming a love. It was beginning to crowd out my affections for the most important love if you're a dad, and that's loving your little girls. And so, fatherhood meant sobriety from 1986 on." I sat on a formal stage inside the New York Hilton, crying in front of strangers, because I realized that this was not a choice my dad had made once; it was a choice he made again and again, day after day. He was talking in a way I had never heard him talk before and revealing himself to me in a totally different way. In that moment, it didn't matter that we were in public. It was just me and my dad.

JENNA

When I was a young girl, my family spent weekends at a lake that was home to alligators. It was good fishing for my dad, but not ideal swimming for my sister and me. Regardless, we loved spending time at the cabin because there were no distractions. It was nature and family. And that was it.

After most dinners, my dad would ask, "Who wants to go on a night walk?" In retrospect, I'm sure he knew how eager I would be to grab a flashlight and conquer the loop around the lake, the thrill of nocturnal alligators in the back of my mind. Sometimes my sister and my mom came along, but often it was just my dad and me. We walked under the moonlight and talked. I don't remember exact details from our conversations twenty-five years ago, but I remember how loved and safe I felt on our adventurous hikes. Those hours of uninterrupted time talking and listening were as precious to him as they were to me. Those night walks are symbolic of how he was as a father: simple, always present, always there.

I think, too, of another walk, one Barbara and I took with him on a brilliantly sunny day in Maine when we were both twenty-three and out of college. The night before, we had celebrated the wedding of one of our cousins, where the guests, including us, grew raucous with hours of open bar and champagne. My dad called us the next morning and asked us to go on a walk, something that had become far more rare now that he was in the White House. Above the sound of the waves and the ocean wind, my dad talked to us about alcoholism. He talked about himself, saying that when he was drinking, he didn't like the person he was becoming. He said that overdrinking ran in our family, and was something that Barbara and I needed to watch out for. I'm sure there are other dads who have spoken like this with their daughters, but I'm sure, too, that many have never had these conversations. I remember being a bit irritated listening that afternoon, nursing a headache and a case of fuzzy mouth. But now I see it as a brave and responsible conversation, one that he could have easily avoided, but didn't. And I think some of the choices I've made in my twenties and thirties stem in part from what my dad said to us on that sunny day.

I can't go on spontaneous walks very often now with my dad; I'm in New York, he's in Texas; there isn't time. But he has found other ways to walk with me.

It's a pretty well-known fact that I come from a line of people for whom pronunciation isn't always a strong suit. My dad in particular was known for getting a bit tongue-tied when he was president. My worst moment was not in that league, but in 2017, I was asked to cohost NBC's red carpet arrival show for Hollywood's Golden Globes. When I was interviewing the indomitable Pharrell Williams, I conflated two Best Picture nominees and called his film *Hidden Fences* instead of *Hidden Figures*. I didn't even know I had said it until after the show; it was a complete slip of the tongue. A slip of the tongue that was made into a meme; a slip of the tongue that produced a lot of Twitter tirades and that hurt people because both films featured the stories of African Americans. I was heartsick over having made that particular mistake, over the knowledge that some viewers thought I didn't care. I apologized the next morning. Waiting on my phone was a text from my dad:

I hear the twitter world is buzzing because of something you said

Here are some thoughts
It is no big deal
Your family loves you which is a lot more important than
  one slip
I made a lot of slips and overall they did not matter
The world is full of people who want to take someone
  down but there are many more people who think you
  are great
So let it go. Be your charming natural self
All will be well
Love you dad

Reminder to myself: Always listen to my dad.

One of the hardest things still for me as a daughter of a for-mer president is having people operate under the expectation that I sit in some kind of judgment of what my father did in his public life. But that's just never how I saw my dad. I have always felt gutted when I've heard him criticized. While I do believe that the decisions he made will ultimately be judged by history, perhaps many different times and with many different outcomes and interpretations, that's not his daughters' role. Our relationship is with the private man, the dad who loves us as his kids, and whom we love in return.

My father jokes with those he loves. His humor is late-night-comic quick and usually self-deprecating. He will never make fun of someone else when he can make fun of himself. When we were rude and disrespectful teenagers, his favorite line was "I love you. There's nothing you can do to make me stop loving you. So stop trying." No matter how deep our disappointment in a broken doll or a playdate or later a test grade or a boy, he would try to pull out a smile or a laugh. And for years we have followed his lead. When we can sense his weariness or crankiness, we make fun of him, joking around until he can no longer help himself—he laughs.

On one particularly long day on the campaign trail in 2004, we were crisscrossing the battleground state of Ohio. Barbara and I were in the car, and we could see complete exhaustion on his face. There was one more rally, one more speech where people were waiting to see him, and as tired as he was, he wouldn't walk out and show the crowd anything but his most enthusiastic self. Barbara and I acted our most juvenile to give him an energy boost. As we drove past the holding area for the waiting press corps, I said that all those reporters had no idea what goes on inside the tinted windows of the limo. And to prove it, I turned around and stuck my tongue out at the window, at the entire press pool waiting behind the rope line. Shaking his head and laughing, my dad said: "Don't do that, Jenna. Someone will take a picture. And there you will be, splashed all over the television screen."

He was right. Like a sheer dress underneath harsh lighting, the limo's windows weren't all that opaque. Everyone outside could see my face and my tongue sticking out. And more than a few photographers captured it for posterity.

A few hours later, while I was running on the treadmill in a hotel gym, I saw my face light up the screen on the local news. Trying to avoid the other patrons, I hid my face and ran from the workout area to get to my dad before anyone else. Commentators spoke about how it epitomized the Bush family's distaste of the media. I can promise you, it wasn't that complicated; it was a moment of a daughter trying to make her dad smile.

Then there was the night, months later, when again Barbara and I noticed that our father was very subdued at dinner. We were living with our parents for a few months, and when we were all in town we made it a priority to sit down together to eat. We hoped it could be like the day in Ohio—jokes, ribbing, and a few moments of sustained silliness that would make him smile and transport him away from whatever burdens he felt. This night, the more we tried poking at our dad, the more he retreated. He looked at his food as he ate; it seemed he couldn't even look at us. And so we tried again, this time fiercely making fun of him: *Dad, you're so grumpy! Old man, what's wrong with you?* But he wouldn't laugh. He'd had enough. He stood up without a word, pushed his chair back, and walked out of the room. We were left staring at each other. I remember feeling hurt—at him for leaving, and at myself for not being able to break the melancholy spell he was under. Later, it was our mom who explained that our dad had just received word that a military helicopter had been brought down in Iraq. It was a large transport helicopter. Every service member on board had been killed.

In the days that followed, he would write notes to each of the families who had lost a son, a husband, a brother. I wonder now that if the look of such life on the faces of his daughters made him think of one of the young men he had read about in his casualty report. Did it make him think about the parents who would never share a meal with their child again? And at those moments, there was also nothing we could do for our dad.

March 10, 2004

Dear Dad,

I had a vivid dream last night, a dream so vivid I woke in tears. Although I am not yet as spiritual as you, I have taken this dream as a sign. You have worked your entire life to give Barbara and me everything we have ever wanted or needed. You have given us love, support, and I know you have included us in every decision you have ever made.

You and Mom have taught us the meaning of unconditional love. I watched as Mom selflessly, gently gave herself to Pa as he suffered. And I watched you give a year of your life to Gampy; I watched your shared pain on election night. At age twenty-two, I finally have learned what that selfless pain must have felt like.

I hate hearing lies about you. I hate when people criticize you. I hate that everybody can't see the person I love and respect, the person that I hope I someday will be like.

It is because of all these reasons that I have decided that if you want me to I would love to work full-time for you in the fall. Please think about it, talk to Mom about it, and get back to me. For now I have stopped applying for jobs in New York. I know I may be a little rough around the edges, but with the proper training I could get people to see the Dad I love.

This may seem like a rushed, impulsive decision, but I have been thinking about it constantly. I want to try to give you something for the twenty-two years you have given me.

In my dream I didn't help you. And I watched somebody win who isn't supposed to. And I cried. I cried for you, for our country, and for my guilt. I don't want my dream to become reality, so if I can help in any way please let me. We can talk more about it during Easter.

I love you and am so proud of you.

Love,
Jenna

Code Name: Twinkle

JENNA

I was at one point in my life a Secret Service detail ditcher. In 1989, as a first grader at Preston Hollow Elementary School in Dallas, I snuck away from my Secret Service agents (and my mom and my sister, who was already buckled into her seat inside our powder-blue minivan) idling in the after-school pickup lane. When April Smith said, "My mom is picking me up at the swings. Want to wait with me?" I hesitated for only a fraction of a second before running straight to the playground. I was eager for April's attention. She was the first grader who boys chased and girls scooted close enough to touch on the reading rug.

April and I soared into the sky, and I dipped my head back, pretending that I had a long, gleaming ponytail like hers. I was admiring how we pumped our legs back under us in perfect unison when I spotted my mom. I knew right away that she was angry. My mother, who almost never runs, was running, pushing back her hair with her hands. The only word she said was, "Jenna," but her stern tone was enough to make my stomach drop.

My mind went into overdrive preparing my alibi, the story that would save me. I barely noticed the other person running up behind her, a man in a suit with sunglasses on. My grandfather had just been elected president. As immediate family, we had Secret Service protection, and the agents had also been out searching for me.

I leaped down from the swing and didn't even wait for her to speak before blurting out, "Mom, I was kidnapped. There was a man in a van with a lollipop, and I got in." It was the clichéd kidnapping story elementary schoolers watched on safety-awareness announcements, and I scrolled back through my "memory" to recount every lurid detail: the sinister man, the promise of candy, and a beat-up van.

I'm not sure if it was the years of listening to other wild tales slip effortlessly out of my mouth, a mother's intuition, or if perhaps my performance wasn't as powerful as I thought, but my mom was suspicious. The problem was that the man now standing beside her wasn't. He looked very serious and intent as he asked me to repeat the story, so I respun the tale of my attempted kidnapping.

"What color was the van?" he asked, pulling out a notepad and pen from his coat.

"Gray," I lied.

"What did the man look like?"

I started to describe a bald man with a beard, and the agent began to wonder aloud if a sketch artist needed to be called. Suddenly, my mom interrupted, suggesting rather firmly that we continue this discussion at home. In our kitchen, it didn't take long for her to extract a full confession. That was not the end of it. She insisted I apologize immediately to the men outside, who were still agonizing over what had happened. I walked out of the house and down our gravel driveway, alone, head bent, even more nervous than I had been at the swings. I tapped tentatively on the tinted window of their black Chevy Suburban. The agent in charge rolled down his window, and I apologized for worrying them by creating the story of my kidnapping.

As elementary schoolers, Barbara and I never questioned the fact that men in suits and sunglasses followed us around. We just accepted it as part of our lives. A decade later, the Secret Service would return.

At dinner parties, over cocktails, when people ask my husband, Henry, and me how we met, we often blush, avoid their eyes, and say, *Oh, at a bar in DC.* We conveniently leave out that we really met in the temporary offices of my dad's presidential reelection campaign. I'm not sure why, except that Henry can still be embarrassed by the bravado others think he must have had to ask me out, and we don't want our gentle love to be defined by something as cold as politics. The truth is we did meet amid the sterile DC office space and rented furniture of my dad's campaign. Because what could be sexier and more conducive to lasting love than a sea of cubicles and young Republicans?

I met Henry on Barbara's and my first day at campaign headquarters. He walked into our office with a friend to be introduced, and then they left to have lunch with Henry's girlfriend.

As they walked away, I looked at Barbara and said, "Of course the one cute guy on the campaign has a girlfriend."

Luckily for me, Henry and his girlfriend broke up soon

thereafter. It would make for a better, more dramatic story if I were their undoing, but I wasn't. In fact, I had pretty much written Henry Hager off, until a month later when Barbara and I invited some friends to the White House to watch a football game. One of the guys worked for Henry, and he wanted to know if he could bring him along. I asked how old Henry was, and he answered, "Four or five years older than us." (The correct answer is three and a half, but no one is counting. Well, besides Henry, who specifically requested that I clarify this.)

And I said, "Oh no, no. I don't want somebody that *old*."

But Henry came anyway, and I had to admit that he was cute, for someone over twenty-five. He clearly didn't hold my youth against me, because he asked me out on a proper date for the following weekend. I said yes, and then he paused and said casually, "Where should I pick you up?" And I replied at the White House because that's where I lived. He took a breath, swallowed, and his voice cracked when he said, "How exactly do I do that? Do I just drive into the gate?" (It's one thing to walk through the pedestrian gate as Henry did that afternoon; it's quite another to drive onto the White House grounds on a solo expedition.) Laughing, I rolled my eyes and said, "Yes, I will give them your information and you just drive in." The evening was already starting to look like that old Hollywood cliché of boy arrives to pick up girl, drives through a few security gates, parks on the South Lawn road, and walks into the residence. What could go wrong?

That day, my parents were out of town, crisscrossing the country in the final weeks of the campaign. It was pouring rain, but Henry was impressively prompt in spite of the weather. I had prepared for our date using proven sources and methods: I followed the advice of the dating bible *The Rules* to always keep a man waiting. Stalling properly, Barbara and I took our time, choosing the perfect outfit, while Henry waited on an uncomfortable settee in the hallway.

I didn't know my parents' schedule, but Henry did. He worked on logistics, and he was getting constant presidential movement updates on his BlackBerry. From the alerts flashing, he saw that my dad was running early, which meant that he would be returning to the White House soon. Preparations were already under way on the South Lawn for the president's arrival. As Henry was escorted into the White House, the officer told him that my parents had landed at Andrews Air Force Base and would be arriving soon on *Marine One*, the presidential helicopter. Henry had parked his car almost exactly where Marine One would land.

In Henry's mind, not only would the helicopter land on his car, or his car would be towed beforehand, but he would also have to meet my dad. He was just a young guy on the campaign. Now he'd have to shake my father's hand and say, "Sir, Mr. President, I'm Henry Hager, and I'm here to take Jenna on a date." He definitely wasn't prepared for that. A casual dinner was about to turn into meet the parents.

When I finally walked out to the hallway, his face flushed. He said, "We have to get out of here, now! Your dad is about to land on my car." I told him it was totally fine. I took my time saying good-bye to Barbara. We headed downstairs and walked through the Diplomatic Reception Room and out the back entrance onto the South Lawn.

The rain had just let up and the smell of the night was fresh. Henry was practically sprinting beside me. Half of him wanted to be a good southern gentleman and walk me to his car, and the other half was telling him to pull out his keys and run. The entire backyard was immersed in final preparations for *Marine One* to land. The rope lines were set, the ambulance and fire truck in place, security at full attention.

We hopped into the car and pulled out just in time to hear the whir of the helicopter blades above. So began my first adventure with the love of my life.

After such a dramatic beginning, you would think that our second date would have been easier. Not so. Henry wanted to showcase his domestic skills, so he offered to cook me homemade pizza at his apartment. (We have since arrived at a more nuanced understanding of the difference between "homemade" and "frozen.")

Once again, he picked me up at the White House, and this time he was more practiced and less nervous. As we drove away, his eyes widened. The fuel gauge was hovering perilously close to empty. He started scanning the road for a gas station, until he finally spotted one at the top of a hill. Then, right when he started up the incline, the tank ran dry, the engine sputtered to a stop, and Henry's car began to roll backward very slowly. He pressed down hard on the brake, but it kept rolling, right into the Secret Service car following behind.

I, of course, behaved like the perfect date and said the very reassuring words, "I am sure it's okay. It's okay, I think," in between muffled laughter.

Fortunately, I don't think Henry even noticed, so complete was his humiliation. He pulled out his insurance and registration. His face looking a bit gray, he got out of the car to speak to the Secret Service agents; that was his first introduction to the men and women who followed me wherever I went. There was no real damage to the Secret Service's massive, fortified Suburban. Henry's Ford Bronco had taken the brunt of it. And he still needed gas.

Henry and I kept dating, and at a certain point he did meet my dad, officially. I guess all boyfriends want to impress the girl's father, but because of who my dad was, the whole process instantly became much more intimidating. Henry, like most guys, just wanted my dad to like him.

The next summer, I traveled to Africa with my mom to support women's health and HIV/AIDS prevention programs, while my dad stayed behind in Washington. Right before we left I said to him, "Why don't you call Henry? He mountain bikes; you mountain bike. Call him and ask him to join you." My dad grumpily replied, "I don't want to call Henry." My mom elbowed him, and he said, "Fine, I'll call Henry." True to his word, he called and invited Henry to go biking with him.

While Henry had a bike, it was an old Schwinn ten-speed, the same bike he'd had in college, the same bike he'd probably had since he was fifteen. But the bike was only one part of the problem.

I didn't mention this to Henry, but mountain biking with my dad was miserable. It wasn't at all relaxing or therapeutic. You couldn't lose yourself in nature to the rhythm of the pedals, because you weren't by yourself. You were surrounded by a fleet of muscular Secret Service agents on bikes. Additionally, a convoy of large, tinted-window black Suburbans followed you, blowing out all kinds of noxious fumes. If you lagged behind, as I did on my inaugural and *only* ride, the Suburbans would pass you. You ended up in what my dad called "the carbon monoxide zone."

A biking expedition with my dad wasn't going to be a pure bonding experience between two men, alone in the woods, getting to know each other; it was going to be two men and a stream of SUVs and about twenty other fit athletes on bikes.

That afternoon, the "Tour del Presidente" had chosen a hilly course. As a pack, they had all sailed down a big hill. Just as they finished a steep upward climb and were about to start the next downhill, Henry's bike chain broke. Of course, my dad didn't stop—he kept riding. When he sped on, the Secret Service riders sped on as well, and so did three or four black Suburbans. Henry quickly fixed his chain and started pedaling as fast as he could to catch up.

As he was racing downhill, Henry realized that the only way he was going to rejoin my dad was to pass two vehicles full of counterassault agents. He had just a four-foot-wide gap through which to navigate. At the exact moment he was passing one of the Suburbans at top speed, a Secret Service agent opened the passenger-side door. For those of you who have never encountered Secret Service vehicles, I should explain that this wasn't an ordinary Chevy Suburban door; these doors are blastproof and weigh hundreds of pounds. You can rip your shoulder trying to push one open. The end of the door caught the end of Henry's handlebars. It was a direct hit. The handlebars turned sideways, stopping the bike, while Henry flew forward, still in biking position, and landed on all fours like a frog.

Miraculously, the only damage was a scratch on his leg and a bruise to his ego—the entire biking crew had witnessed the whole thing. Henry finished the ride, certain it was part of a bigger plan to get him out of the picture. I remember calling my dad from Africa and asking, "How was biking with Henry?" And he said, "Well, he's a nice kid. The biking was fun. It was all good until he was doored."

The President's Toast
Jenna and Henry's Wedding

May 10, 2008

Before I call on Jenna, I would like to offer a toast.

There's one caveat: I'm an emotional wreck. So welcome. First, I'd like to toast the family. We are so blessed to have a great family.

The Hagers and the Bushes. Second to our friends. I've learned in life you can't make it without your friends. So to all our friends, thanks for coming.

Every parent's desire is to raise a soul who is a contributing, decent, compassionate person.

So part of my toast goes to the Hagers for raising such a decent, compassionate man. And thanks for teaching him how to fish. And ride bikes. It's about time.

So I was in Saudi Arabia and I was telling the King how fired up I was for my daughter's wedding. And the King of Saudi Arabia says, "What's her name." And I said, "Jenna."

Whereupon a member of the King's court said, "That's interesting. 'Jenna' in Saudi colloquialism means 'bounties after the rain on the desert.'"

I can't think of a more fitting description.

After the rains there is freshness, an energy. There is unparalleled beauty. And the greatest sight is (or there is great excitement) when the birds sing.

I love you, darling.

Staying on Script

BARBARA

The thing most people don't immediately see about the presidency is how scripted every public moment is. Who stands or sits where, how long the Marine band plays, the precise moment when the president stands and walks to the podium; everything is scheduled and choreographed. Ballets seem freeform by comparison. Even private meetings are governed by protocol, but the public moments can feel like a full-on soundstage production. That same attention to every detail also governs travel, inside and outside the United States. Everything has to be perfect because so many people are watching.

Whenever I traveled overseas with my parents, it was written in my schedule book what type of outfit I would need to plan for each event as well as the instruction that I would walk up the stairs of *Air Force One* behind my father, and that at the top he would pause and turn around and wave. On landing, there was an entire greeting protocol: My father and mother would walk down first; Jenna, if she was also traveling with us, and I would follow behind. Waiting on the tarmac would be the American ambassador and often the head of state of that particular nation, along with an entire delegation of other dignitaries, arranged in descending order of importance, plus a press pen filming and photographing away.

I had to be "on" from the moment I passed through the doorway, even though I had spent the entire transcontinental flight sitting around in my sweatpants, ankles swelling. Before the plane began its final descent, I would transform (or try to transform) into a well-dressed daughter, blowing out my now-droopy hair over the cabin sink. The feeling of performing never quite went away. After hours of travel and time-zone jumping, being "on" didn't come so naturally. I would always worry if I was doing the right thing, keeping one eye on my parents for cues. So I did know not to curtsy when I met the Queen of England (American citizens do not need to), but not that I should never lightly touch Prince Philip when we were being organized for a group photograph. Oops. I took the photographers' directions to "get closer" a little too far and learned the hard way. The Queen, in her long, beaded formal dress and perfectly placed crown, was even more gracious than you'd expect—a TV-character Queen. I was somewhat tongue-tied, asking only about her visit to the United States, her family, and her dogs, unsure what one should ask a queen. Afterward, I kicked myself. I'm sure thousands of people have felt the same way after shaking hands with my dad in a long receiving line.

In Italy in 2001, I accompanied my parents to the Vatican to meet Pope John Paul II. I followed the strict dress code and wore long black sleeves, but I was allowed to leave my hair un-covered because I was still considered a girl. We were ushered in and my breath was taken away as we walked through the enormous, intricate, sacred Vatican to reach our meeting room. While the tourists got to pause and look around, we were rushed through elaborate spaces. There was only a set amount of time on the schedule allowed for walking. After we arrived at our papal audience, I tried my best to focus on the con-versation while also slyly glancing around, hoping to absorb every detail. Sadly, we saw the Pope late in his reign—when Parkinson's had taken hold of his body and his ability to com-municate had been hampered. With a clock and twenty other people in the room, there was no time for me to say much of anything. The questions I wish I could have asked—what were his hobbies, his regrets, his passions, who did he miss the most—would have been met with silence as he was hardly able to speak.

But the few times we stepped outside the strict official pro-tocol, it was a very different story.

On a trip to Italy in 2006, to accompany American athletes to the Olympic Winter Games, my mother and I had a private lunch with Silvio Berlusconi, the Italian prime minister. Al-most immediately, Berlusconi, who had a reputation as a ladies' man, began calling me "Bella" and musing over my blue eyes. He told me that I should have children with his son, right after telling me, "If I was younger, I'd have children with you." A few sentences after that, the female translator stopped translating.

Then there was the one night I will puzzle over for the rest of my life, a night in the summer of 2008, when I found my-self in Maine at Walker's Point at the same time as Russian head of state Vladimir Putin. During my dad's presidency, no other heads of state were invited to Walker's Point (minus Sarkozy, who stopped by in shorts to say hi, as his family was vacationing and boating nearby). Putin stayed in my great-grandmother's house across the street, barely fifty feet from the main house's front door. It is the house my aunt and cousins stay in—and one I've stayed in myself. The invitation to Walker's Point was intentional, designed to be a chance for Dad and Putin to talk about missile defense in Poland in a re-laxed setting. (Russia was opposed; Dad was pressing that the missiles were meant to protect Europe from Iran and were not being directed at Russia.) My father, Gampy, and Putin had been out on a boat fishing—the Russian president caught the only fish.

I arrived with my mom for dinner in the familiar dining room, in a white linen dress and my hair still wet from a day in the ocean. Like every other dinner, Gampy was at the head of the table, but this time there were two interpreters and Secretary of State Condoleezza Rice. Putin came dressed for Maine, a collared polo shirt beneath a sports jacket. The meal was messy lobster. And as the table-seating gods would have it, I was seated near President Vladimir Putin.

My mind froze. What does one say to make small talk at dinner, especially when one does not speak Russian? I asked about his two daughters, both talented musicians living in Moscow. I needed another line of conversation, so I asked, "President Putin, do you have any siblings?" "No," came his reply. I had an image in my mind of big Russian families, like the endless nests of brightly painted matryoshka dolls, and so I said, "Wow. You're an only child?"

"No. I had a brother, but never knew him. He died before

I was born." And in English, without a translator, Putin told me the story of his family's life before his birth. His father, a Russian soldier, had fought against the Nazis during World War II on the frigid battlefields near what was then Leningrad and is now once again St. Petersburg. After being injured by a grenade thrown directly at him by a Nazi soldier, Putin's father struggled to safety and eventually managed to reach a hospital. The Putin family already had a son, Putin's older brother, who had been born during the war. But food was scarce and conditions were terrible. Leningrad was being starved. The Putins' baby was taken from his home and placed in a form of foster care, where he became ill and died. The Putins never laid eyes on their child again. Putin's mother, mourning her son, returned home and fell ill. In the bitter cold, death was rampant. Russian medics with carts moved from building to building, removing dead bodies and rolling them off for burial. Putin's mother's limp body was added to the cart. Walking home, Putin's father saw his wife, and saw her take a shallow breath. He pleaded to keep her, to which the medic replied, "That's just more work—we'll have to come back for her dead body soon." But Putin's father prevailed. He carried his wife back to their frigid home. She survived and after the war gave birth to a second baby boy, Vladimir Putin. "And so," said the Russian prime minister, "I have no siblings."

Perhaps my favorite international journey was the last one I took with my dad, to the Olympics in Beijing. We knew before we landed, as the US media often reported, that electronic devices would likely be bugged and each room probably had a listening device. We didn't bring our cell phones.

I'd wake up at 3 a.m. with terrible jet lag and wander into the suite's living room for breakfast, only to find my dad doing the same thing. Punchy from lack of sleep, we laughed hysterically, knowing we needed to keep our conversation to the most mundane topics, such as please pass the cereal. Everything else had to be pantomimed, which made for many moments of muffled laughter as my dad, my uncle Marvin, and I played a three-way game of charades. One time we returned to the hotel and found three men in Marvin's bathroom, fixing "something." Were they really fixing something, or adjusting a listening device or retrieving a tape of our shared conversation? We will never know.

During that trip, my father spent time with many of the American athletes. The US men's basketball team wanted my dad to stop by before a game. I went with him and stood in the huddle next to LeBron James, Kobe Bryant, and Jason Kidd—these giant, athletic stars—feeling like a doll-sized miniature. My dad looked over as I was wedged next to LeBron for a photo and said, "She's your little mascot." And for some reason, these iconic basketball players started laughing and calling me "our little mascot." I'm sure they've long since forgotten, but I never will. When I'm ninety, I'll still remember the day when I was, however briefly, a US Olympic basketball team mascot.

Don't Go. Stay Here.

JENNA

My first kiss was in the fourth grade during a game of spin the bottle played in my friend Lindsay's backyard. It was also the first coed party I had ever been invited to. I had spent the afternoon leading up to it lying on the white fluffy carpet in my bedroom, listening to Wilson Phillips on my purple CD player, and scanning the pages of an Archie comic book, searching for an outfit inspiration from the raven-haired, daringly dressed Veronica and the somewhat preppy, perky blond Betty. (I probably ended up wearing something I had worn to school earlier that week.)

Lindsay seemed worldly to me; she had an older sister and her parents were puppeteers. Adding to the aura of preteen sophistication, the party was at night. All the guests were prompt, and by the time the sun had barely dimmed, we were standing in the backyard. The boys and girls had clustered on opposite sides of the patio, divided by anxiety and opportunity.

Egged on by Lindsay's older sister and the fact that the boys were fifth graders, we agreed to play spin the bottle, a game so daring we had only heard of it on television. The big glass bottle would rotate around the circle and slowly stop. One by one, couples ran behind a bush and then returned, blushing and laughing. I was kissed by John Henderson, who was enough of a gentleman to ask me to rollerblade with him to 7-Eleven before moving on to greener pastures and a prettier girl named Catherine. (In the perfect postscript to fourth-grade spin the bottle, he recently messaged me on Twitter!)

I recovered from that first encounter, but dating and boys didn't seem to become any less confusing as I grew older. There was the middle school boyfriend who gave me a cute silver frog ring on a horse carriage ride in Central Park when we went on a class trip. Was he the prince? There was an older high school boyfriend whom I adored. We would talk late into the night, on my own phone line. It was a secret we shared. He asked me to the prom, and I went on a special trip to Dallas with my mom to search for the perfect dress. I finally settled on a long black sequined gown that I hung expectantly in my closet. I had circled the date on my calendar. Then my boyfriend and I had a rocky week, and he disinvited me. He flew in a beautiful girl, who had already graduated from Austin High, to be his date. I stayed home. Eventually, my dad convinced me to put on the dress and play a CD, and we danced around the governor's mansion living room, our own makeshift prom.

In college, I faced an entirely new set of complications. Dating in general can be awkward. Dating while men pretending to be college students, dressed in khaki pants and carrying backpacks and the occasional fanny pack, followed me in black Suburbans was not all that fun. I always felt a hint of embarrassment when I brought a new date around. Was I being subtly judged? If I went out with a few boys, was I playing the field? All of this led me to stay in an imperfect relationship for too long. I continued to date one college boy for years, even after he kissed another girl in front of my face.

When I was twenty-three, I met Henry Hager. He is six foot four, so there was almost no way not to notice him when he walked into an office at my dad's campaign headquarters in Washington, DC. I'm fortunate that he also noticed me. We survived our first hilarious dates. Pretty fast, I was smitten with him, and I hoped he was smitten with me too.

I invited him to a White House Christmas party. At one point when we were dancing, most likely caught up in the festive spirit, he whispered, "I love you." He blushed; instead of playing it cool, he had inadvertently let the words slip. But I took those three words and ran with them. I said, "I know! Let's get married!" At which point, Henry turned bright red. We had been dating for three months.

But there were two not-so-small truths that led to my desire to get married: I did love him, and I had been steeped in my own parents' crazy love story, which was a whirlwind. For years, Barbara and I heard stories of how our dad went to Maine to visit his parents about a month after he met our mom, and as soon as he arrived, he was already on the phone, trying desperately to reach her. When he heard that she wasn't home, he left Kennebunkport and got on a plane back to Texas because he couldn't stand to be away from her and didn't want her to fall in love with someone else. He proposed barely six weeks later and they were married in three months. I had heard the stories for so many years that I basically assumed I would follow the same romantic path, never mind that my parents were turning thirty-one during their romance and I was twenty-three.

Henry is rational and levelheaded. He didn't propose after six weeks or three months, and we continued to date over an entire blissful winter. It was my first long winter on the East Coast, and I often went out without a jacket; I didn't even feel the cold. The next winter, I said to a fellow teacher that it seemed frigid, and she replied that the previous winter had been worse. I hadn't noticed. All I could feel was the heat and happiness coming from Henry. We dated all of 2005 and into 2006. I was teaching, and Henry was working for the Department of Commerce. Then came the moment of truth: Henry was going to go back to the University of Virginia to get his business degree and I had decided to move to Latin America to work for UNICEF.

Except I hadn't quite decided. I said to Henry, "I won't go to Latin America if you propose; I will stay here." Almost every time Henry would say something sweet, such as, "Oh, I can't believe we're going to be apart," my response was to raise the stakes: "If you propose to me, we won't have to be apart. I will just cancel my plans."

This had been our running dialogue when one random Tuesday in early May, Henry suggested that we go to dinner. But this wasn't a "Let's grab a burger or a salad" dinner. He had made reservations at Asia Nora, which was a well-known downtown restaurant in DC across from the Ritz-Carlton hotel, and he asked me to meet him there. I started thinking: *It's fancy; it's a Tuesday; I have school; a lot of thought has gone into this date.* It was also very unusual for us to go out to a fancy din-ncr, and definitely not in the middle of the week. And it was not long before I was supposed to leave for Latin America. So even before the hostess showed us to our table and handed us our menus, it felt like an occasion.

Asia Nora was known for many things, but one of its signature creations was homemade fortune cookies. You could call the restaurant and get the fortune personalized. Henry had read about this and thought it would be romantic to have one made for me.

Over organic Asian food, our conversation was light and full of laughter. The entrée plates had been cleared; we were at the end of the meal, finishing chocolate mousse, when out came a server with two glasses of champagne. Henry Hager is many things, but he is not a champagne guy. And did I mention it was a Tuesday? As I stared across the table at Henry, whose face looked perplexed, I noticed that tied to my champagne glass was a little piece of paper. The paper looked just like what you might find inside a fortune cookie. I uncurled the piece and read in tiny typed letters: "Don't go. Stay here." The miniature message could mean only one thing: Henry was proposing, and that was exactly what I said.

Now Henry looked worried. His next words were "Wait! What? No, no!"

It turned out that Asia Nora either ran out of cookies or Henry didn't call early enough, because instead of having a piece of paper inside a cookie, they had used champagne glasses. More than that, they had messed up the message. Henry had told them to write, "Go, and when you come back, I'll be right here." It had been dramatically shortened to: "Don't go. Stay here."

So, I'm sitting at a table, in a public restaurant, saying, "Are you proposing?" while Henry is shaking his head furiously and saying, "No, no." He couldn't get the words out fast enough. He kept trying to tell me, "This was supposed to be a fortune cookie and they got it wrong. This is the wrong message."

The whole event was a lot like those posters that you use to teach kids about emotions: I started off shocked, surprised, happy, saying, "Yes, yes, I will marry you." And then I realized he was not asking, so I was mortified, and then angry, followed by hysterical laughter. After that, it was "Check, please. As fast as possible."

When your dad is in the White House, it's not just you and your boyfriend having a conversation in a restaurant. It's you, your boyfriend, and every other patron within earshot. (Thankfully, this was about two years before the advent of the smartphone.) The two women sitting next to us called the *Washington Post* and relayed the whole moment, including, apparently, their views of what we ate. So two mornings later, I awoke to a write-up in the Reliable Source, the gossip column in the *Post*'s Style section.

A Champagne Bottle Was Popped, the Question Was Not

> *Jenna Bush* has been stepping out with *Henry Hager* for a year and a half now, a point when any young couple might start mulling questions about the future, so it's natural if there was maybe a little *frisson* as they sat down to dinner Tuesday at Asia Nora.
>
> The 24-year-old teacher (beaded light-green tunic, dark slacks) and her beau (who turns 28 next week) ordered a lavish meal, fellow patrons said. Then, as they shared a chocolate mousse, the wait

> staff brought champagne—Jenna's flute with a mys-
> terious note taped to the bottom. She read it and
> burst out laughing. "I thought you were proposing!"
> she hollered. "I nearly [soiled] my pants!"
>
> Who knows what the note said; witnesses gleaned
> that it was an inside joke Henry wanted to deliver in
> a fortune cookie but didn't get ordered in time. The
> restaurant's not saying.

I don't remember actually saying any of that. I also didn't stop to think about people listening. But whatever I did or didn't say or do, the story, as reported by "witnesses," lives on in the *Washington Post* archives. Asia Nora closed a little over a year later, and although still not yet betrothed, Henry and I remained happily together.

It was the summer of 2007, and Henry and I joined my family at Camp David, the presidential retreat, for the weekend around the Fourth of July. At Camp David, everyone has their own little cabin. The first evening, when Barbara was in her cabin, Henry called her, asking if she was alone and if she could talk.

Barbara wondered why her sister's boyfriend wanted to have a heart-to-heart. Henry said, "I'm going to tell your dad I want to marry Jenna, but I wanted to make sure it was all right with you." This is why I adore Henry. He knows me well enough to realize that my heart is intertwined with Barbara's. He wanted her blessing first.

The next day, Barbara and I and Henry and a few friends who were visiting were going to watch a movie. The only ones who weren't going to watch were my parents. Just as we were about to sit down, Henry said, "I don't feel that well."

I rolled my eyes in a slightly unsympathetic way and said, "Why, what's wrong?"

Henry said his stomach hurt. He went back to his cabin while we started the movie. And by now his stomach had really started to hurt. He was planning to ask my dad for his permission to marry me while we were distracted by the movie. Right away, he called my dad's cabin and asked to walk over to speak to President Bush. In the background he heard my dad say that he was napping and to tell him to come by in about an hour and a half. Henry put on the television to watch tennis. He started pacing back and forth in the cabin. By now, his stomach was tied in macramé knots. He found a Bible next to the door and started reading it, hoping there would be some sort of miraculous intervention.

Finally, around 3 p.m., he walked over to my dad's cabin, rehearsing the speech he had prepared. He and my dad sat outside on the deck, the mountains in the distance. Henry is a steady, slow talker, and he had his opening statement and his supporting points all laid out. He nervously began, "Sir, I want to marry your daughter. I love her and these are the reasons that I know I could take care of her—" My impatient dad interrupted right away: "Nope, I don't need the reasons. Let's get Laura out here." He started yelling, "Laura, Henry's proposing!"

I think, truth be told, my dad was relieved to have me off his hands. He ended his talk with Henry saying, "We love Jenna, but you know she can be a pain in the ass." By the way, Dad, if you are reading this, I don't really appreciate it even all these years later. So poor Henry never got to list all his well-thought-out reasons, because my dad didn't need them. He knew my solid, kind, rational Henry was the perfect person for me.

After "proposing" to Barbara and my dad, Henry didn't ask me that weekend at Camp David. He didn't propose to me for a month. Everyone in my family knew what was coming except me. We had planned a road trip in Maine from my grandparents' house up to Acadia National Park, and we were going to be camping out for a week. Our final destination was Cadillac Mountain, the highest point along the North Atlantic seaboard and one of the first places in the US to see the sun each morning. Henry told me he wanted us to be on the top of Cadillac Mountain for the sunrise.

After a few nights of camping and rigorous hiking, I was exhausted and easily irritated (a pain in the ass, perhaps?). And now Henry wanted us to wake up at 4 a.m. I texted Barbara to complain about the early wake-up. I complained so much that Barbara told my mom, "I'm not sure if he's going to end up asking Jenna."

But I got up at 4 a.m., and Henry and I hiked. We reached the top of the mountain as the sun rose, and Henry proposed to me at sunrise, as the first rays appeared on the horizon.

It was the best yes of my life. In fact, I had chosen Henry Hager years before in a cubicle, in a temporary office. I was so sure of our love, I had tried to propose to him at a Christmas party years before. So as we watched the sun rise over the Atlantic Ocean, an ocean I had swum in every summer of my life, I knew I had a new definition of home: Henry.

And if the witnesses this time heard everything we said, they never said a word. All that my Secret Service detail said afterward was "Congratulations. We are very happy for you." Although I do think they were probably glad that we got married on the flat ground at my parents' ranch in May, not after another summer hike up a mountain.

Dearest dazzlingest Beast and newly born "Henry Beast,"

Happy, happy, happiest wedding! I would like to properly welcome Henry to his "Beasthood." How exciting to have a new bro and a married sis! Guess what this means...? A lifetime of more snuggling with arguments over who's the ham and who's the cheese...a lifetime of fun exploring and trips...A lifetime of Henry's belly talking...and a lifetime of Love and Fun! Beast—you have been a wonderful, quirky, loving, and brilliant partner; and Beast, you have filled my life with millions of great memories (including those from when we were roasting in the womb). I know if ever in trouble, our twin powers can unite! And I can't wait to have Henry as a new addition. Henry—I can assure you that the Beast will make your life more joyful and love-filled than you know! I can't wait for all the adventures and fun you two will have! I love you cats more than tongue can tell!

Love,
Barbara

The Mythology of Love

BARBARA

Growing up, we were steeped in a mythology of love. Our parents' love story was the first: They grew up in Midland, played in the same park; attended, briefly, the same junior high; but never met. They lived in the same apartment complex in Houston, but never met. Our mom's best friend married our dad's best friend, yet still they didn't meet (my dad had to miss the wedding). At age thirty, they were finally introduced at a barbecue in Jan and Joey O'Neill's backyard. Their first official date was miniature golf. Three months later they were married, Midland's "old maid" and Midland's "most eligible young bachelor," although they were both thirty-one. It was a lightning-strike romance. We heard the story often as kids, until we could tell it as if it were our own. Cinderella and Snow White with their Prince Charmings were one thing; our parents were a real-life fairy tale, living fated parallel lives set amid the wind-whipped mesquite and tumbleweeds of West Texas.

Our family mythologies stretched even further back. Harold

Welch and Jenna Hawkins were set up on a blind date in El Paso, Texas, where they paid six cents to walk across the footbridge to go dancing at the Tivoli nightclub in Juarez, Mexico. The next day, the local paper reported: "Last night, Jenna Hawkins was seen dancing with a handsome stranger." They were married in the chapel at Fort Bliss right before Pa left for war. Ganny and Gampy's was also a wartime wedding. But what I didn't know until I was grown was that they also were each other's first kiss. On a visit to Maine, over dinner surrounded by aunts, uncles, and cousins, I asked my grandfather if he remembered meeting Ganny for the first time. Of course he did. He was at a holiday dance, looked across the room, and saw a girl wearing a striped skirt. She was absolutely the most beautiful girl he had ever seen, so he asked a friend who she was. "Oh," came the answer, "that's Barbara Pierce." As Gampy tells it, Barbara had gone to the dance with some guy nicknamed "Liver Lips." To this day none of us know Liver Lips's real name, because the point is that George H. W. Bush asked her to dance, and Liver Lips was soon forgotten. Barbara Pierce was sixteen. They were married in 1945 when she was nineteen and he was twenty, while Gampy was back briefly on leave from flying planes in the Pacific theater in World War II.

My grandmother becomes softer and gentler around her husband of more than seven decades. In the last few years, she has willed him back from the brink of death in the intensive care unit several times. His obituary had been written, but Ganny wouldn't let him die. She even chuckled when she heard that Gampy's dear friend Jim Baker smuggled in a thermos of dry martinis and a pack of pork rinds. In her eyes, George H. W. Bush can do no wrong. And she can do no wrong in his. At ninety-two and ninety-three, they sleep holding hands.

I have heard every variation of the question: "Why aren't you married?" My answer is always the same: "If I wanted to be married, I would be." I've had wonderful partners, but there was always too much work to do, too much of the world to be seen.

Like many women, when I was younger, I assumed I would get married. In high school, on the long bus rides across stretches of flat Texas highway to play in soccer games, my friends and I would huddle together, knee-to-knee in our seats, our shin guards and cleats clacking, as we listened to a Sony discman play Dire Straits's "Romeo and Juliet" on repeat, laughing as we asked out loud, "I wonder what our husbands are doing right now."

With my own high school loves, I'd reread every text I received on my tiny brick-shaped Nokia phone. There were very few texts because it was brand-new technology in 1998, a time when the fact that we had caller ID on our landline was cutting-edge. I'd analyze each word, wondering if a question about homework was somehow indicative of a deeper bond, not yet recognizing that I would one day move beyond the ups and downs of teenage infatuation.

Or perhaps it took my own growing up to understand that love looks many ways and takes many forms.

Fairy tales are all about the beginnings, with five words tacked on: "They lived happily ever after." There is nothing about the middle, where in the case of Ganny and Gampy, your beloved daughter dies; and nothing about the ending, about the one who is left behind to carry on. The last Christmas Grammee was strong enough to travel, she joined us at my parents' Crawford ranch, staying in Jenna's room, next to mine. At night I slept with my door open, listening in case Grammee needed anything. In the dark, I woke to her quietly and frantically calling my grandfather's name—"Harold, Harold." I found her standing next to the bed, her unsteady feet holding up her tiny, silk-pajamaed birdlike frame. She gazed at me uncomprehendingly, and asked, "Where's Harold?" I didn't have the heart to tell her he was dead, instead hoping that for just a second, she could believe he was only down the hall, returning soon. So that's what I said. As I tucked her back into bed, she said, "My feet are cold. When I sleep, I press my feet against Harold so he can keep them warm." By then, Pa had been gone for fifteen years, and yet in the dark, cold night she was still just a touch away from his presence, from snuggling her feet against the warmth of his legs.

Or perhaps it is that there are so many ways to love.

In New York, it's always a surprise to ride the subway on Ash Wednesday. For one day, hundreds of people walk around with an ash cross in the middle of their foreheads, and suddenly an intimate, profound belief of a complete stranger is shared. When I had my first devastating heartbreak in my early thirties, I'd ride the subway, wondering if anyone could see that inside my chest, my heart was torn in two. And when my heart hurt so badly I couldn't help but wonder how many other people riding the subway felt the same, how many others were wandering the city with broken hearts.

My dad was the first person I called after that breakup. I don't know why—I never shared much about my relationships with him. I'm private like my mother. But through it all, struggling to hold the belief that someone could be wonderful, while also understanding you shouldn't build the rest of your life with them, I relied on my dad. And daily, he would call or text. Just to check in, just to share the burden with me. He didn't make promises of things getting better or the relationship ultimately working out, but he just shared that while my heart hurt now, it would not always feel that way. Every morning I would wake to a text from him, just saying hi, his usual "love you, baby," and in a small way, affirming that heartbreak hurts and that is okay.

I picked up the pieces, but he never stopped texting every morning. Every night, I read a meditation—a short modern-day interpretation of a Christian Bible verse, meant as a form of silent prayer—before I doze off. And every morning he rereads the same meditation from the same book, texting me the verse, which he has illustrated by emojis. I text back my own emoji picture. It is short. And it is daily, 5:30 a.m. Texas time, 6:30 a.m. New York time, waiting there for me when I open my eyes. It is so simple, and yet it is everything.

So it is at age thirty-five that I am at last ready to write my own mythology of love. It is not based on legends of white dresses and rings and bouquets; it is rather the comfort of what is shared with another soul. It need not be any kind of romance; it is simply the bonds that we form, the way our lives interlace with one another, the unexpected ways we find to care. My first trip to Uganda, I visited a health clinic where a mother had brought her fragile, ill daughter, wearing a lavender dress and looking like an angel. I spent less than an hour in that clinic, but those thirty to forty minutes changed my life and my life's direction. That mother's choice to love her daughter, to make her beautiful, to hope that her life might be spared by drugs to treat HIV/AIDS, led me to my love of working around the globe to improve health care. In my work, I have been able to surround myself with caring humans, those who actively choose love for one another over division and fear. Today, they are the ones rewriting the rules and the myths of love.

I look into the faces of the people I see: family, friends, colleagues, strangers, and I know that we are all, each of us, born to be someone's love story.

E-mail from Jenna to Barbara

Sister cat! Meow!

Happy Valentine's Day (early)—remember the early bird gets the worm. But it is you—the sister cat—who gets the prestigious first sister prize of the Americas! Congrats!

You received (and were nominated) for this award that will keep your peers' eyes filled with an awe-inducing jealous stare because you have succeeded in completing all 20,003 of the requirements! Yippee!

Basically—you are the best, most beautiful, courageous, silly, funny, sunny fabulous sister in the whole globe. Thanks for inviting me and my stinky friends to Yale. You truly deserve this extremely important award! Wear this with pride! I heart you, sister.

In Front of the Camera

JENNA

I used to run from the press, literally sprint in the opposite direction. When I lived in DC, on beautiful days I often drove from the elementary school where I taught to my parents' house so I could run along the National Mall. It was my favorite way to unwind, except for one perilous passing: through the White House gates. News correspondents were often milling about on the grounds, waiting to do television stand-ups along the North Lawn. To me, it sometimes felt as if I were an animal in a safari park, trying to stay out of range of prying eyes and long lenses. When David Gregory, NBC's six-foot-five reporter, spotted me once and waved, I dropped my head and yelled, "Run!" to a friend jogging with me.

It turns out that my sprinting wasn't very effective. Years later, when I joined the *Today Show*, one of the first things correspondent Amy Robach said was that she had been part of the White House press pool that traveled to Texas when I married Henry. As an NBC reporter, Savannah Guthrie spent part of that weekend reporting from in front of hay bales in a Crawford, Texas, parking lot. She did a story on other reporters "gobbling" up details about my wedding cake, and she even visited the Yellow Rose store to pick up a Jenna and Henry mouse pad (which, you probably won't be shocked to learn, she no longer has). Now Savannah is not only my colleague, she is my next-door neighbor, and our daughters are dear friends. A woman I would have run from ten years ago if I had seen her on the steps of the White House is one of my best friends. I cannot think of a better lesson of how life can take unexpected turns.

My early experiences with reading my name in the bold print of the tabloids left me feeling exposed and vulnerable. Every time a camera shutter clicked during my freshman year of college, my stomach sank. I even dreaded the short walk across the South Lawn to the helicopter to Camp David, with all the photographers and camerapeople penned off behind the rope line, shouting questions—imagine being waylaid by an aggressive, nosy neighbor every time you step out the front door. One time when I was feeling particularly disheveled, a sweet man on the White House residence staff, Sam, saw how miserable I looked and offered to hold up a garment bag so the photographers couldn't take pictures of me. I said yes, but then they just filmed and photographed me walking behind a garment bag, with my ankles sticking out of my sandal-clad feet. The photos looked even more ridiculous than if I had just walked across the grass.

After the underage-drinking episode at Chuy's, I remember someone telling me that Meredith Vieira on *The View* had criticized us for our indiscretion. I was hurt, thinking, *Doesn't she have kids? Doesn't she know that people aren't perfect?* When I first went on the *Today Show*, I was nervous to be interviewed by her, worried that she viewed me one way—simply based on something she had said while chatting on live TV. And yet, almost a decade later, I worked with her and I adored her. I also understood far better how she could have looked at the situation and had a strong reaction; I was able to see her side, but it took me a while to get there.

Two years after college, I moved to Latin America to work for UNICEF. For the first time since 2000, I lived a life completely away from the headlines, television screens, photos, and prying eyes. My job was to travel around the region, meet mothers and their children, and write their stories for UNICEF. I didn't realize the satisfaction I would get from telling the stories of the people I met. What struck me, too, was how eager they were to share their lives, how grateful they were to have someone listen, be interested, and write down everything they had to say as if it truly mattered, which to me it did.

One story that touched me deeply was that of a seventeen-year-old girl named Ana. She was so young, but she had already lived a difficult life: She was an orphan; her mom, dad, and a sister had all died of HIV/AIDS. Her sister first, then her mother when Ana was three, and then finally her father when she was in sixth grade. Ana had been born with HIV as well, but she had survived. When I met her, she had left the home of her abusive grandparents, had a newborn baby, and had quit high school. She lived in a small makeshift house under a scavenged tin roof with her daughter and her boyfriend. For nine months, I talked with her every day. I knew every painful, difficult detail about her life, but I was embarrassed to tell her one crucial thing about mine. In the beginning, I had wanted her to feel comfortable, so I simply introduced myself as Jenna. I never told her my last name or whose daughter I was. As she had told me her stories and her lineage, I realized I had to tell her mine.

Every morning over coffee, I would write in my journal: "Today is the day!" But I kept putting it off, uncertain about how Ana would react; wondering if I could ever just be Jenna, her friend, again. When I finally did tell her who I was and who my family was, her face lit up and she laughed. I had worried for no reason. She didn't care at all. Because she already knew me, and she knew I cared about her. Our friendship was what defined us, not my name. She saw all of me, all of my sides, not just one.

What I did have because of my name was a unique platform to tell Ana's story. With her permission, I wrote it as a book. To promote the book, I did interviews with TV personalities including Diane Sawyer and Ellen DeGeneres. I was happy to talk about Ana. There were even times when television "got" me. Ellen DeGeneres had me pull a prank on my dad and call him at the White House. I also did a segment on the *Today Show* and by the end, I was surprised to discover that I actually enjoyed doing TV.

But when the book tour ended, if you had asked me if I would be working in the media in ten years, I would have told you emphatically, "No way!" With an exclamation point. If you had asked me if I would work with the same group of people that had once plastered those hideous freshman-fifteen pictures of me everywhere, the answer would be no!

One of the *Today Show* executives called me and asked if I was interested in being a correspondent. *Today* may have been ready to give me a tryout opportunity, but I wasn't ready to try out for them. I had a job teaching at the SEED school in Baltimore, which I loved. I was newly married, and I hadn't studied journalism. I didn't even have time to watch the *Today Show*. I said, "Thank you, but no." Periodically, though, I would hear that they were still interested. When they called again in 2009, I went up to New York to see what they were proposing.

I sat down with Jim Bell, the executive producer, in a room with comfy director's chairs, and he showed me a highlight reel of *Today Show* moments—and at the end of the video of all of the best moments there was a picture of me. When I walked back into his office, I was unexpectedly greeted by my future NBC family: Brian Williams, Meredith Vieira, Matt Lauer, and Al Roker. They were sitting in a semicircle, and I wasn't sure if this was a welcome-to-the-media meeting or an intervention.

I was completely overwhelmed. When they said, "What questions do you have for us?" I couldn't think of a single one. I began to sweat. Fortunately, they asked me what I wanted to do, and I said that I wanted to tell stories. I wanted to tell education stories, women's issues stories, and every response was, "Great. We'll let you do that." It was as if anything that I wanted to do was possible; it felt like taking the job was the right thing. I started out just sticking my toe into the water. I kept teaching part-time in Baltimore and then racing to take the train up to New York to prepare my segments.

The job wasn't easy. I knew the basic outline: I had to get up early, sometimes at 4 a.m., to be on the set, and on the weeks that I was preparing segments, I traveled across the country reporting. But *Today* did give me the opportunity to tell stories, which I loved, especially those of ordinary people who are making an extraordinary difference. I've also had the chance to sing karaoke with Céline Dion, had members of One Direction question if I was a cougar, and develop incredible friendships.

I'm often asked to pick my most meaningful interview. It is hard to choose just one, but a favorite of mine was with the late poet Maya Angelou. We spoke about her memoir of her mother. After the camera stopped rolling, I stayed to chat with her. Sitting across from her at the antique wooden table in the kitchen of her Harlem brownstone, I asked for her advice: *What's the best way to parent?* She was older, relied on an oxygen tank, and often had to take breaks. She spoke about how her mother had many jobs, and brought "little Maya" along to learn and experience everything. When she became a mom herself, a single mom, she had that same adventurous attitude. As I listened to her thoughts on unconditional love and independence, I touched my pregnant belly, wondering what type of mother I would be. Could I raise a strong woman? Sadly, Maya Angelou died a year after we spoke.

When I started at *Today*, I knew how I wanted to conduct interviews. I understood how it felt when someone had interviewed me and arrived with an open mind, versus when the interviewer had a preconceived notion about who I was before I ever said a word. I remembered all the times I had been typecast as the loud one or the wild one or the shallow one, sometimes just because it was easier or faster than trying to get to know the real person. I knew what it was like to be asked questions that made me deeply uncomfortable or were based on assumptions about my parents or my grandparents. I didn't want to do those types of interviews. I wanted to capture the true essence of who people are.

Ironically, there were times when I brought the media spotlight to the White House. On a few occasions, I interviewed First Lady Michelle Obama for the *Today Show*. The place where I had run from cameras was now the place I was returning to, with camera crew in tow. As we approached 1600 Pennsylvania Avenue, the crew asked me for directions—how to get to the right gate. I had no idea where to go. In my twelve years in and out of this famous address, I had never been to the press gate, only the smaller personal gate on another side of the building. I also had never been to the White House briefing room.

After I finally arrived at the right entrance, some of the ushers, who had been there with my parents and even my grandparents, were waiting to give me a hug and to ask if I wanted my usual, oatmeal and a latte. I couldn't make myself that comfortable; I had gone to Starbucks with the rest of the crew.

We set up to interview Mrs. Obama in the Blue Room, the same room where my mom had done so many interviews when she was first lady. When we sat down, Mrs. Obama asked me if I wanted to go upstairs and see my old room. I was worried that I wouldn't look professional, so I said no, but I thought it was so generous to ask.

It was the period when much of the press was focused on Mrs. Obama's arms and her fashion styles. I wasn't going to

ask her about any of that. Her strength reminded me of my
grandmother, and her grace reminded me of my mom, and I
hoped people would see through the camera all the sides of
her that I saw. (When I posted a photo of the two of us on
Instagram, I had to remove some unkind comments below,
saddened that just because our families came from two different political parties some believed we couldn't share things
in common.) I hoped I could help viewers to see that beyond any titles, there are real families and real people who
live in this home called the White House. But the difference
was, that didn't just have to be my hope. Sitting in the interviewer's chair, it was now my job to talk to Mrs. Obama in a
way where I could do just that.

Following our first interview, we became periodic pen pals,
writing each other letters every once in a while, such as when
my babies were born. After the 2016 election, I reached out
to her, thanking her for her service, asking for advice about
how to talk to my daughters. She wrote back, saying: "One of
the many gifts I have received from my tenure as First Lady
is getting to know you and Barbara...and of course your mom
and dad. You all are wonderful people who Barack and I love,
respect, and admire."

Many of my colleagues say that their biggest fear is leaving
an interview without having asked the tough questions. My
biggest fear is that I won't represent the person I'm interviewing accurately, that I won't show who they really are. I
never want them to come across as one-dimensional. That's
true for me as well. Whether I am in front of the camera or
away from it, I am the same person, living an unscripted life.

Political DNA

BARBARA

By sixth grade, I was a nonconformist conformist. Like most thirteen-year-olds, my style had gone AWOL. The most prized piece in my wardrobe was a raspberry velvet Jessica McClintock dress with an attached pearl choker—my favorite feature. Only I could make a Jessica McClintock dress look Goth. I wore it anytime I wanted to look chic (let's define "chic" very loosely), until the velvet took on a balding sheen from too much dry cleaning. Beneath it, my legs were nicked but had been strategically Band-Aided following my novice clumsiness with a razor.

My daring was limited to slumber party antics that never got past the planning stages. We would hatch elaborate plots to dress up in black and toilet-paper another middle schooler's house, but by midnight, we would fall asleep in our "criminal gear" before we could sneak out. In other words, there were no early clues that I was anything but docile, eager to be more mischievous than I was, in spite of a very real obsession with vamp nail polish and Courtney Love.

So it must have come as a bit of a surprise to my parents when I started to discover and voice my own strongly held opinions. At the dinner table, I argued against the death penalty over my mom's chicken and rice, feeling my way around a newly formed opinion, one that differed from my parents'. By high school, I passionately supported gay rights.

In seventh grade, I met my best friend, Matthew, a wild, hilarious, artistic, tie-dye-wearing eighth grader, full of a whole lot of not caring what other people thought. Our older family friends from New York City had sent Jenna and me the aforementioned Chanel vamp nail polish for our birthday. We were ecstatic—did this somehow make us city girls? Matthew commented on my nails in the hallways of St. Andrews and a friendship, now lasting twenty-two years, was born. We hung out every chance we could, lazing the summer away jumping on his trampoline or listening to Tori Amos. I always assumed Matthew was gay, I just never knew if he'd be comfortable enough to share it.

One night during our sophomore year of high school, we lay in the dark talking on Austin's public golf course. After thirty minutes of stumbling and small-talking, of trying to share, Matthew came out to me. I was not surprised by his news, but I was surprised by his fear. His worry of being accepted. His worry of what others would think. Everybody knew Matthew. Everybody loved Matthew. Nothing would change. Or would it?

My first attempt to broach the subject of gay rights with my dad was a particularly heated debate that ended with my storming away from the table. With the absolute certainty that comes when you are sixteen, I believed that one conversation would be all it took to change my father's mind. My dad, to his credit, kept his calm and simply asked me questions to understand my thought process. Usually the fastest eater at the table, when he is deep in thought, my dad slows down. That night, he almost stopped eating as we had our back-and-forth, him asking, me insisting. I knew my dad as accepting and tolerant. Unlike me, though, he was not comfortable with the idea of gay marriage and its implications. In retrospect, I realize that with those questions, he was helping me to hone my argument, or at least to think out loud as I went along. Healthy family debating was surely in effect. That said, I was not entirely unsuccessful. During a brief pause, my mother interjected, with a slight raise of her eyebrows, "It looks like your daughter has backed you into a corner." My dad may not have changed his mind that evening, but neither did he try to change mine. We didn't end up in a bitter relationship-ending feud; rather, we started a dialogue with each other that would continue for years to come.

Perhaps to most people there is an expectation that policies and opinions will be passed down in political families like eye color and height, encoded in our shared DNA. Or that party loyalty is interwoven or even synonymous with family loyalty. While that may be true for some families, it isn't true for ours. Our dinner table never resembled a Model UN conference or a game of Risk; we don't analyze obscure congressional races. On the contrary, we are a freewheeling, not always polite, ask questions, and explain your point of view type of family. We are a bunch who can't quite be pigeonholed, probably in the same vein that any famous actor's family can't be painted as dramatizing Shakespeare at every gathering. We adhere to the "time and place model," which lots of times means apolitical conversations. My dad can, and has, sat down to a meal with a restorer of antique barns and spent the entire time asking him about the preservation process. We talk books, sports, movies, and health care in Rwanda, not to mention relationships and the more mundane details of what is going on in our lives. Twice a year, like clockwork, someone invariably retells the story of my dad and Uncle Marvin's epic tennis game in the 1970s where they ended up in a fight—a line call argument that has persisted for decades. Whether the ball was out or in remains unresolved. Undisputed, my dad jumped over the net, chasing Marvin up a nearby fence where he waited in fear. In that way, our dinner table is a lot like tens of thousands of others: toggling between interesting and insular.

Even the concept of politics as a family business doesn't quite fit. I suppose there will be more Bushes who may want to run for elective office, but, early on, despite a failed run for Congress, the business our dad most wanted to follow his dad into wasn't even the presidency, it was baseball. Gampy was a college baseball player whose Yale team made it to the College World Series in 1947 and 1948. As captain of Yale's baseball team, he greeted the legendary Yankee Babe Ruth when the Babe came to Yale to donate a signed copy of his autobiography to the campus library. Gampy passed on his love of the game to my dad. As a little kid in Midland, dad would play baseball for hours in the yard and read over the inning-by-inning box scores of Gampy's college games, which Ganny had neatly recorded as she sat in the stands. Although he loved Little League and sandlot ball, my dad's love (or talent, depending on who you ask) wasn't enough to make him pro-anything on a major-league team. Instead, he translated this shared love to the business side.

Even if politics is not our universally shared family vocation, however, none of us can completely avoid living a political life. One day in DC, as Jenna and I were leaving the gym, we spotted a bumper sticker slapped across the back of a car. We would have missed it had we gotten there twenty minutes later or parked in a different spot or just looked the other way. But we didn't. It was white on black, with a red Texas flag, and informed us, "Somewhere in Texas a village is missing its idiot." Well, that idiot was our dad. For a second, the words stung, but then we looked at each other and burst into unstoppable laughter. While it was awful to us, it was also funny—bravo to that joke writer. Now this line comes up regularly when we want to rib our former-leader-of-the-free-world father: "Well, somewhere in Texas a village is missing its idiot…"

That moment also underscores how from the beginning our political lives involved a unique type of choice regarding the negativity—to be upset or to laugh it off. It was up to us to decide how we would react. In a way, being forged in that environment helped us figure out the issues that mattered most to us—the ones that rose above the noise of pundits, tabloids, and political commentaries; the ideas we just couldn't get off our minds.

Another assumption is that because you come from a political family, you can somehow sway a parent's (or Congress's) decisions or serve as the perfect vehicle to deliver a message. In one humanities class at Yale, I received mediocre grade after mediocre grade no matter how hard I tried on my papers. I nervously signed up for office hours with my TA to get to the bottom of what I was doing wrong. She replied she'd give me an A if I convinced my father not to go to war in Iraq. Whoa there. I was unsure how to respond to her insinuation that my phone call home would somehow sway an entire government, that my twenty-year-old opinion would have affected anything. We were not political pawns. I didn't drop the course, but I was left with the profound discomfort of wondering how many other people thought a presidential daughter should be held responsible for any beliefs other than her own.

How do you find your own voice when you come from a public family, where people are asked to comment on everything from trade policy to their favorite flavors of ice cream? How do you go about speaking in *your* authentic voice? How do you stake out what matters to *you*? I started down my own public path in 2011. That year, I was asked to make a brief video in support of gay marriage. I had reached an age, twenty-nine, when my friends were getting married; my own sister had already wed. I believed all my friends should be able to marry, straight or gay. I wanted Matthew to be able to marry. It was an issue that spoke to my core beliefs. Julianne Moore and Whoopi Goldberg had made videos before me. I looked theirs up on YouTube and saw that they had about seventy views each. I'm camera-shy, I don't love extra attention, but a few views on YouTube didn't seem like such a big deal. What I didn't realize was that as the daughter of a former president who had publicly opposed gay marriage, this video was going to be a big deal. The video was covered on the front page of the *New York Times* and made its way to the backseat TVs of thousands of NYC taxis—I'd climb in and see my face speaking out, "Everyone should have the right to marry the person they love," right after a Sandy Kenyon movie review. My video received more than 520,000 views on YouTube.

I was unprepared for the number of casual friends, passing acquaintances, and even perfect strangers who would stop and congratulate me, adding, "How very brave." Or go so far as to say, "How very brave of you to betray your family by speaking your beliefs." I would flash a passive smile, but underneath I gritted my teeth. To me, betrayal is the worst thing you can do to another person. Cross that with family and it's incomprehensible. My parents have never felt betrayed by anything I have said or done. It wasn't in any way an act of bravery—I was following the basic guidance my parents had given me: Raise your voice when something is important to you. I was being a good daughter, politics aside.

My dad knew I was interested in filming the video beforehand, and he was supportive because it was what I believed was right. Dad is motivated by the concept that "to whom much is given, much is expected." It was because of him that I was given a voice, even if I was using my voice to speak out on an issue upon which we differed in opinion. For him, it meant he had done his job as a father. In the years since, I've periodically spoken on other issues, including global health and Planned Parenthood; I've even been to the occasional political fund-raiser.

I'd like to think that may be my ultimate family DNA: Be true to your heart. It's harder than ever to talk about politics these days. If you love someone, sharing different political views shouldn't be seen as a personal betrayal. Rather, it's a chance to hear and consider your loved one's point of view, while still maintaining your own beliefs. Do not fear doing what you believe is the right thing regardless of who is listening in the wings (or even the West Wing, in my case).

E-mail to Barbara from Gampy

Yes, here I am. The old Gampster who is missing you more than tongue can tell.

But I am happy you're happy. I am also pleased you met the Ruperts.

The Gampster is still in Houston. Tonight we go to A&M where tomorrow Justice Scalia will be speaking at the library. Then in the afternoon I come back to my office where I will meet up with my new brother, POTUS 42. We will jointly do a taping for TODAY show and then go out to Westside Tennis club where, before cheering thousands, we will close out the successful Bush Clinton fund.

I have enjoyed working with President Clinton. He has been pleasant about your dad and has avoided a lot of chances to take shots at the administration.

I greatly respect your AIDS work with the kids. I don't think I could handle the sadness. I would, I am afraid, leap ahead of Doro as Captain of the family Bawl Team.

What happened to Bird Man. Has he been officially dumped?

Yes I will be seeing Johan Rupert in Germany at month's end. I think I am hitchhiking a ride on his plane from Moscow to Geneva.

I have been travelling constantly and I am tired, slightly grumpy, and ailing—cold at first, then allergies, almost flu. "Tired" is the key word here as I whine on; but the good news is we will be in Kport Friday afternoon for keeps.

Tommy, Michele, Ariel, Sadie, and Don are all on

the point as I type. Paula and Alicia fly up with us on Friday morning. Excitement on my part is overflowing. It's like when you fill the tub to the top. Then climb in and the water runs over the sides of the tub. Well that's how excited I am about being back on the "point" and sleeping in that cold air, the waves rocking me into the arms of Morpheus her ownself. Or is it his ownself?

I miss you terribly. I really do.

The Enforcer

JENNA

At ninety-two, Barbara Bush still writes letters. When my Ganny is cross, or when she is pleased, for that matter, she can't help but tell you, often in print. Her most recent letter to me arrived typed, its geometric letters practically jumping off the stark white page. From the first sentence, I knew she was angry.

That summer we had visited my grandparents in Maine and I'd organized a family tennis tournament. The teams were open to anyone, and as the organizer, hoping for a dramatic run to the finals, I picked the local tennis pro to be my partner. Sure enough, we prevailed over the other teams of cousins, uncles, and my aunt Doro. The stage was set for the deciding match against my dear cousin Wendy and her dad, Craig. A dozen family members and a few family friends came out to watch, waiting for some good or at least some entertaining tennis.

I put on a show. After missing a shot, I dropped down to the clay court to display my athleticism: doing first a plank and then a push-up. When I hit a particularly impressive shot, I did the worm—a body-shaking dance move where I shimmied along the ground—and received lots of cheers. After my partner and I won a game, I lifted my skirt to the audience and shook my huge tennis underpants.

The person egging me on the most? My father. He cheered, "That's my girl!" He triggered a chorus of audience laughter, until I was running around the court, dancing a made-up jig and yelling: "Not today!" My partner and I lost the match, but I felt like I had won: In the bright summer sunlight, I had made *some* of the people I love most laugh.

Within a few weeks, Maine was long forgotten, the memories faded like the tans on our shoulders. I was back in New York, my mind occupied with the demands of work and children. I stood at my kitchen counter opening mail. Among the flyers and bills, I saw an envelope with my grandmother's familiar, loopy cursive. In it was a typed note addressed to both my dad and me. Like a lawyer building her case, Ganny recited my every unsportsmanlike infraction, from lifting my skirt to the cheers I had chosen to yell in the heat of the moment. And what was worse, in her eyes, was that I had done it all in front of my mom, my daughters, family guests, and most of all, Gampy, who had been raised with the highest standards of sportsmanship. She pointed out that Gampy's own mother, who was an avid athlete, a gracious (not to mention *great!*) tennis player, and a self-effacing woman, would have despised a display like mine. Ganny was deeply disappointed with me because of my behavior, and angry that my dad had encouraged it.

And that is my grandmother: exacting and determined to protect the ones she loves. My audacity had embarrassed

Ganny; she thought her husband deserved a less juvenile display. I'm in my thirties, but my grandmother's words and reprimands can still sting, making me tear up and sniffle like a child. She had added a handwritten postscript: *Throw this letter away. Don't mention this again!* I dutifully tore up the pages as she'd ordered, but the thought that I had disappointed my precious grandfather was too much to bear.

There have been many other Ganny letters over the years, full of love, sometimes disdain, and always protective to the core. She is a woman of high standards but also fierce loyalty. If she believes you are in the right, she will defend you without reservation.

In the spring of 2001, Ganny had herself received a critical letter in the mail. Barbara and I had just been caught for underage drinking. In the note, a friend of my mom's pleaded with my grandmother to intervene and do something about our wild ways. My grandmother read the letter, and then furiously and impulsively penned one back, stating that her granddaughters were doing just fine, that we studied hard and we wanted to do good. She ended with her own zinger: If this woman were a true friend, she should support my mother and mind her own damn business. The Enforcer was doing what she does best: Enforcing! Protecting!

People stop me all the time—in airports, grocery stores, on the sidewalk—to tell me how much they adore my grandmother. One woman recently came up to me as I was boarding a flight and said, "I always dreamed of having a grandmother like yours! She seems like the type of woman who bakes amazing cookies." I laughed. I can honestly say that I have never tasted a cookie made by my grandmother. Or a cake, or a pie. I cannot remember Barbara Bush ever baking anything.

Is it her appearance—her neat sweater sets accessorized with pearls; or that stiffly styled, signature white hair—that makes people think of my grandmother as a domestic maven, a throwback to an earlier, far more deferential time? My Ganny—I can assure you—is a thoroughly modern woman. She has always been blunt. As first lady, she was vocal about things that could have made her unpopular. She came out as pro-choice, having an opinion different from her husband's, the person she adores most in the world. In 1989, two months after she became first lady, she toured Grandma's House, a care center for infants and small children with AIDS. There, at a time when many people were still terrified of the disease, she purposely held a baby, kissed a toddler, and hugged a grown woman, all diagnosed with HIV/AIDS, trying to break the deep stigma associated with the disease.

In private and in public, she speaks her mind, sometimes the very first thought that comes into it. During the 1984 presidential campaign, Ganny was asked to describe the Democratic vice presidential candidate, Geraldine Ferraro, and she replied that the word she would use "rhymes with rich." (Gampy and Gerry later became friends.) Twenty-four years later, she said of Republican vice presidential candidate Sarah Palin, "I sat next to her once, thought she was beautiful, and I think she's very happy in Alaska. And I hope she'll stay there."

She's also more than willing to say what she thinks within her own family. On one visit when my dad put his feet up on her coffee table, she told him, "I don't care if you are the president of the United States, take your feet off my coffee table." And my dad did. When Jon Meacham, Gampy's biographer, earnestly asked her on the back porch at Walker's Point if she had ever anticipated her son George becoming president, her answer was to laugh until she had tears in her eyes, and then answer with a resounding "No." If one of us says something smart, her favorite reply is, "Well, that's using your head for something other than a hat rack!"

Her love of animals is the stuff of family legend. She particularly loves her latest dog, Mini, who has bitten almost everyone in the family. So great is her loyalty to her four-legged companion that if someone tries to pet Mini and Mini bites, she will almost always defend Mini.

But Ganny also has a very tender side. For years she has enjoyed needlepointing, making Christmas stockings for the entire family. Now she is making a stocking reserve, so that all the great-grandchildren, including any who might be born after she passes away, will have a Ganny stocking to hang for Santa. She has even made a plan to have someone else personalize them if she is no longer able.

Ganny, who married at nineteen, is an explorer. When my grandfather graduated from college they packed up their new baby, George, and drove their red Studebaker from Connecticut to West Texas, where they rented a duplex. The house at least had an indoor bathroom—most of the houses on the block had outhouses—but they had to share it with the residents on the other side of the house, a mother and a daughter who made their living as prostitutes. It must have been quite an experience for Ganny, who had grown up under the huge old oaks in Rye, New York, and was married in a white satin dress with eight bridesmaids. In the next few years, she would move with her husband to Bakersfield, California, and then back to West Texas, to Midland, where the surrounding towns had names like Notrees, meaning there wasn't even one tree poking up from the ground.

When my grandmother was in her sixties, she decided she would take her granddaughters, when they reached sixteen, on their own adventure. The two of them would travel to anywhere in the world they wanted. When our turn came, together, of course, since we were twins, Barbara and I chose Italy. We had never been to Europe, and we dreamed of star-filled nights and dining on pasta in piazzas. The three of us did stroll through museums, ruins, and cathedrals, and rode in a gondola, but in Venice, Ganny also took us to the famous Harry's Bar, announced that it was cocktail hour, and proceeded to buy us our first martini. With each sip, we felt closer to adulthood.

I didn't quite realize it then, but Ganny had met Gampy, the love of her life, when she was that same age, sixteen. By the age of twenty-eight, Ganny had already lost her mother in a car accident, given birth to three children, and buried one of them, Robin, who died of leukemia when she was only three. When I was twenty-eight, I was barely a newlywed. Today, my Ganny remembers not the sorrow, but the wonderful feeling of her darling daughter's "fat little arms around my neck." After Robin died, my grandfather wrote to his own mother that he liked "to think of Robin as though she were a part, a living part, of our vital and energetic and wonderful family of men and Bar. Bar and I wonder how long this will go on. We hope we will feel this genuine closeness when we are 83 and 82." And they still do, at ninety-three and ninety-two.

But there was a time when the sadness almost broke my grandmother, until she heard my then seven-year-old dad solemnly telling his friends he had to go inside because he needed to play with his mom. After that, she insisted everyone get out and live life, herself included. All those summers in the water, sand, and garden in Maine are as much a legacy of that determination as they are of her love of the outdoors.

I'm not sure if Ganny was tough before or if she became tough because of her early married life, living far from her family and far from everything she knew, grieving alone in dry, dusty West Texas. When at night I tuck in my blond, blue-eyed daughters—girls my dad says look like Robin once did—I cannot imagine how my grandmother found the strength to pass her own daughter's empty bed. But by the time I got to know her, Ganny's strength was so powerful it had truly become a force, a life force for those of us who know her.

For years, one of her favorite places to be has been in her garden at Walker's Point, planting, weeding, and pruning. I think of her like my childhood picture-book character, Miss Rumphius, who planted fields of lupine to make the world a more beautiful place. Today, Ganny, who is unsteady on her legs, rides around on a scooter, inspecting the landscaping, looking for places that need to be thinned or cleaned out, spots to add new plantings, all to ensure that Walker's Point will be even more beautiful after she is gone.

At night when we all gather for dinner, she still sits, as she always has, close to her husband. When someone says something particularly funny, she will laugh uproariously. Then she will look over at Gampy, who does not hear as well as she does, and will quickly add, "Say it again; say it again, please, so that Gampy can hear it too."

When I look in the mirror now, I see bits of my mother's features and recognize the sound of her Texas twang. But a lot of times when I speak, it's my grandmother, my strong, impulsively hilarious grandmother, whose voice I hear.

Rational Dreamer

BARBARA

I never thought I would launch an organization; that was something other people did. In fact, it was my slightly bossy twin, Jenna, who first insisted I do so.

The official start of my story began when Jenna attended an AIDS and Young Leaders conference hosted by UNAIDS and Google. But in truth it began long before that. Jenna and I grew up in the age of AIDS; the disease was first identified in the United States the year before we were born. We were eight when Ryan White, the American teenager who became one of AIDS' poster children, died. We were eleven when the first HIV drug cocktail was introduced. And we were twenty-one when our father launched PEPFAR, the President's Emergency Plan for AIDS Relief, to deliver HIV/AIDS medications to the continent of Africa, home of the greatest concentration of infections in the world.

I had traveled with my parents to East Africa when

PEPFAR was launched. It's the greatest of clichés to say that my eyes were opened, but they were. Uganda, where we first landed, was a feast for the senses. The colors were vibrant and the energy and motion enthralling. The cities were alive with an entrepreneurial spirit, people opening makeshift stalls and selling items on almost every street corner, with traffic and pedestrians converging in a great surge toward their destinations. Standing in the midst of it, I had an overwhelming sense that I, too, needed to get moving, that I should be racing forward with my own life.

As the days passed, my eyes were opened in another way. In sparse, freshly scrubbed clinics (it was a presidential visit after all), I saw the opposite of this vibrancy. I saw wasting and the skeletal descent toward death. I saw lives that did not have to end, and a disease that could be halted by getting medicine to those in need. Hundreds of people waited in lines in the streets for drugs that had been readily available for years in the West—though in the US, we were still dealing with the harsh stigma associated with HIV/AIDS and the complexity of accessing health care, it was becoming increasingly rare to see Americans affected by the disease looking like walking skeletons. Rather, they were thriving physically. The tool keeping people alive—antiretroviral drugs—wasn't readily accessible on the African continent. This was infuriating to my twenty-one-year-old mind—how could we live in a world where medicines existed but weren't distributed to places considered "poor" or "complicated"? I felt like I had to be part of something—small or large—to ensure that people around the world were treated fairly, which meant access to medicines and care that could and would save their lives. Once I knew HIV drugs existed, I couldn't look away.

After college, I worked in the Red Cross Children's Hospital in South Africa and for UNICEF in Botswana. I completed my assignments, I received my performance reviews, and then I flew back home. But I wanted to do more.

For the next few years, I worked in New York, which I loved. I read the news, I went to speeches, I kept up with the latest in global health, although I didn't know where this knowledge would lead. Until the day in 2008 when my sister called me from the aids2031 conference. She was in the audience when the head of UNAIDS (and one of the researchers who discovered Ebola in the 1970s), Peter Piot, challenged the room to engage our generation in solving global health issues. One of her tablemates raised his hand and suggested a Teach For America–like model for global health. Jenna called, excited, because she had heard me mention a similar concept.

A few weeks later, I headed to Jenna's home in Baltimore to meet a few of the conference attendees for the weekend. We had no intention of starting an organization—it was just a group of global health nerds excited to share ideas. We ate sushi, sang karaoke, and drew on whiteboards. From that weekend, Global Health Corps (GHC) was born. The idea was in fact modeled a bit on Teach For America: Recruit creative, committed twenty-somethings and place them in settings where they are immersed in the challenges of healthcare delivery, becoming innovators and problem solvers. It was Jenna who pressed her global-minded sis to pack her bags.

We started with the idea that today's challenges—whether the water crisis in Flint, Michigan, or Zika—won't be solved by a smartphone, but by smart people: These problems require human intervention. Our second idea was equally straightforward: We believe that health is a human right. Our vision was people and patients at the center, with creative systems designed to serve them. And we wanted everyone learning: an American learning from a Rwandan learning from a Haitian. The premise was that GHC teams would always pair two different nationalities, for example, a Nigerian and an American working together on a project in Newark, New Jersey, because each would bring a different perspective and a fresh set of eyes.

But while our ideas were big, Global Health Corps started small. It began as a gamble; we had two staff members, including me. I had quit my safe teaching job at the Cooper Hewitt Museum, and GHC had a scant two months' worth of funding in the bank. In the beginning, one of my GHC partners, Jonny, would regularly spend the night under the table in our "office"—a donated conference room—because we were working around the clock. It was convenient, really, but scared the hell out of the first person walking into our office every morning—greeted by Jonny popping out from under the table.

In 2009, we opened applications for our first class of fellows—young people focused on using their minds and creativity to improve health-care delivery in underserved parts of the world. We weren't sure if anyone would apply—we were "a community of young leaders," but we were few in number—a brand-new organization with poor branding and no track record. Yet the opportunity to serve and use nontraditional skills to solve problems appealed to the almost one thousand young people who applied. We picked twenty-two inaugural fellows to build GHC with us. Being in this together made us braver than we ever imagined we could be. Looking back, I can hardly believe we grew from such a fledgling operation to where we are today. Our team is twenty times that size now, and our global community of fellows and alumni is nearly nine hundred strong—and while we still sleep in bunk beds on travels, no one sleeps under a table anymore. We recruit high-potential people, age twenty-one to thirty, from around the world to work on the front lines of health equity in Malawi, Rwanda, Uganda, the United States, and Zambia—and each year almost six thousand people apply for 140 positions. About one-third of our fellows work in major US cities—because if you believe that global health is a problem that only happens in other countries, you are mistaken. For many years, statistics have shown that one out of every twenty people living in Washington, DC, is HIV-positive.

We try not to divide the world by what's happening in each country. GHC consciously avoids using terms like "I," and perhaps most importantly, "us" and "them." The world is becoming only more global, and the only way problems will be solved is if all of us, and I mean the global "us," are in it together. Our projects reflect our diversity and the many possible avenues to solve problems. Our fellows may work inside government ministries or develop mobile apps to improve data collection. Some are researching the impact of unintended pregnancy, some are working to increase access to midwives, and others are teaching about childhood nutrition. It is a roll-up-your-shirtsleeves-and-dive-in type of work.

So what kind of people become GHC fellows? The ones who qualify share an impressive amount of grit. One of the grittiest was Ameet Salvi. I first met Ameet at GHC's inaugural training program—he was twenty-six years old and had left a stable job to go to Zanzibar. He graduated from UC Berkeley with a degree in engineering and had been using his engineering brain as a supply-chain expert at the Gap, the large clothing retailer (supply chains are how products are produced and transported to reach consumers). He'd always been social justice–oriented, but he hadn't found a way to apply his practical business skills to serving others. Once he joined GHC, Ameet's task was to do for the one million people living on the island of Zanzibar exactly what he had done for Gap. But instead of working to get the season's hottest jeans and T-shirts into stores, Ameet used his skills to get lifesaving medicines to health clinics—and into the hands of the patients who needed them most. (In Tanzania, like many places in the world, drug shortfalls are frequent. A mother might take her sick child to a health clinic and learn he has malaria, only to be told that the medication for malaria is not in stock at the local pharmacy. Suddenly, that preventable illness becomes a death sentence.) Ameet took a chance on GHC, and it took his life in a direction he couldn't have predicted—that of a global health advocate. He stayed in East Africa after his fellowship, and when the Ebola crisis erupted, Ameet moved to Sierra Leone to be part of halting its spread. He now works as the director of operations for Partners In Health in Sierra Leone.

A couple of years ago, someone described GHC to me as a crew of "rational dreamers"—people who believe the world can and should be made better and then go about connecting the dots, putting in the sweat every day to make that dream a reality. Each summer, as they wrap up their year of service, all the fellows gather alongside a body of water, the Indian Ocean in Tanzania or the Nile River in Uganda, and share their stories of impact and failure. A few years back, I sat on the breezy bank of the Nile River with Temie Giwa, one of our fellows from Nigeria, who is a passionate women's health advocate and a great example of a rational dreamer. When I first met her, she seemed quiet, likely feeling the impostor syndrome that most of our fellows do on day one. Now I was listening to her share her personal story. When Temie gave birth, there were complications. She was in desperate need of blood, but there was no blood to be had because Nigeria did not have blood banks. Temie and her baby survived, and from there she made it her singular mission to start a system of blood banks in Nigeria so that other mothers and their babies might be saved. She had to change minds and overcome a culture that was rightfully fearful of donating and sharing blood because of the risks from AIDS. She could have easily walked away with a healthy baby; instead, she works every day so other mothers never have to face the obstacles or know the fear that she experienced.

My initial impression of Temie was wrong—she is not quiet, she is fierce, singularly focused on solving a seemingly insurmountable problem. It brings me to tears of both inspiration and pride every time I read an article or receive an e-mail update from her. Temie's story is just one of almost nine hundred—our interconnected family (#GHCfam) who have chosen to wake up and see opportunities to serve rather than be debilitated by problems. In my own bit of rational dreaming, I can't help but wonder what the world will look like when there are thousands of Ameets and Temies working alongside one another in the unglamorous, but critical, middle ground of health systems.

———————

Ironically, for people who come from a family of homebodies, my sister and I have chosen careers where we travel often: she in front of the camera; me most often tucked away on another continent and hard to find. My work with Global Health Corps means I spend more time on a plane than at home, en route to East or Southern Africa, Europe, and crossing the United States. Some people think international development is all about glamorous treks through rural areas in Land Rovers and meeting with ambassadors. While that might be the experience of some, my own experience has differed, instead riding a bus with my partners on the bumpy roads of Butaro, Rwanda, to see the lifesaving work of our fellows at Partners In Health. Or sleeping on bunk beds with my colleagues in Kigali as we struggled to open our first African office, not knowing if anyone was going to apply to GHC, but hoping they would.

As much as I travel, I still find magic with each trip, but a kind of magic that feels more like a blessing of tranquillity. Where I once was overwhelmed with the physical beauty of new places, now the breadth of that beauty includes the people I know from my travels and the closeness that we feel. When I land in Rwanda, I know which taxi drivers I'll recognize at the airport; I know who is waiting for me in the city and the countryside—hundreds of people, as many as I know in New York. They are my community. Some of them have even become my second family. Our first Rwandan hire is "my brother," and me his "sister"; in Uganda, there is another Barbara who works with GHC, whom we all call Mama B. They both come to my apartment in New York and know my cat, Eleanor. A year can go by without any of us being in the same room, but once we are together, it is as if no time has passed. We trust each other in every way. We are each other's leap of faith.

Along with the people, I have discovered another type of beauty: When I stand in parts of Tanzania or Zambia, I feel as if I am looking through a glass all the way back to Texas— where I can see the same expanses of yellow, dried grasses, red sands, and clusters of spruce trees. I now know that the places I have been have led me full circle, back to a renewed love of home.

More Than Tongue Can Tell

JENNA

On his eighty-eighth birthday, I interviewed my grandfather for the *Today Show*. I did it outside at Walker's Point in Maine. It is his favorite spot, the place where he has gone nearly every summer since he was born. Gampy calls this home his "anchor to windward." I was sitting with my grandfather in a place that held his history, his heart, and mine.

Gampy seldom talks about himself. He's never been one to tell "war stories" or recount his accomplishments in government and politics. So I started off by asking him the obvious questions about his life and being a young man fighting in World War II. He had ignored his dad's advice to go to college right out of high school and enlisted instead. He became the youngest naval aviator to date, at age eighteen. As we were talking, I forgot the lights or the cameras, or why I was even there. I looked over at him, really looked, and I saw his paper-thin, vein-lined skin, the wrinkles and spots marking a life well lived. The man who had stood at my wedding was now in a wheelchair. I felt compelled to ask my grandfather something I might otherwise have been afraid to—I veered from my carefully typed list of questions and I asked him if he had ever thought about death.

He answered without any hesitation. "Yes, I think about it. I used to be afraid. I used to be scared of dying. I used to worry about death. But now in some ways I look forward to it." And I started crying. I managed to choke out, "Well, why? What do you look forward to?" And he said, "Well, when I die, I'm going to be reunited with these people that I've lost." And I asked who he hoped to see. He replied, "I hope I see Robin, and I hope I see my mom. I haven't yet figured it out if it will be Robin as the three-year-old that she was, this kind of chubby, vivacious child, or if she'll come as a middle-aged woman, an older woman." And then he said, "I hope she's the three-year-old." Robin was the daughter this giant of a man lost years before to leukemia. The little girl he held tightly, who spoke the phrase I have heard Gampy repeat for my entire life, forever knitting Robin's voice into the tightly woven fabric of our family: "I love you more than tongue can tell."

Six months later, we almost lost Gampy.

It was Christmas Eve and I was in Richmond, Virginia, with my in-laws. We were just sitting down to dinner when my mom called. She didn't waste any time. She told me that Gampy wasn't doing well and that Henry and I had to come to Houston. We needed to go—now—to say good-bye. She had booked Henry and me on a flight early the next morning.

I sat down to dinner, passing festive plates of holiday ham and wiping my eyes. My in-laws were comforting, but I alternated between feeling terrible about ruining the meal and excusing myself to go into the bathroom and cry. More than anything, I wished Barbara were there.

The next morning, my parents and Barbara picked us up at the airport. It was a relief to see Barbara's face, and I held her hand as we rode to the hospital. During the car ride we all spoke of our determination to make it a good day: "Okay, we aren't going to cry." My father, a notorious tear-shedder, was firm about all of us holding our emotions in check, saying it again and again, until I realized that what I was hearing was his own inner monologue. My dad had already written his father's eulogy.

I was almost five months pregnant with my first child, Mila, who was barely a round bump, and the first thing Gampy did as we walked to the bedside was reach out his shaking hand and touch my stomach. And then he said, "There's death and there's life and I can't wait to meet this baby." Barbara grabbed me to steady me, but I still started to cry, and so did Henry and my dad and my mom, because we all believed that there was no way our Gampy was going to meet my baby. My grandmother, sitting in a chair a few feet away, asked: "Why are you crying? What do you have to cry about? He can't wait to meet the baby. He's going to meet the baby." Awash with hormones, I couldn't stop sobbing, and I had to leave the room to regain composure. When I came back, Ganny was still saying how "Gampy can't wait to meet the baby" and "Gampy can't wait to be at the library opening" for the dedication of my dad's presidential library. She was sitting there by his bedside, as she had done nonstop since he was first brought to the hospital. As she sat, her hands were in constant motion, needlepointing a Christmas stocking for my unborn child.

We nodded our heads, and I thought, *Poor Ganny*. It was abundantly clear that everyone except her knew the truth. The only explanation was that my grandparents' lives were so intertwined that she couldn't face life without him.

In retrospect, it was in fact a memorable day. But not in the way any of us had planned. We've always called my grandmother "the Enforcer," and on this Christmas, she just wouldn't give up. She kept stating over and over again all the things that Gampy had to look forward to. She gave him no choice but to live. And so he did.

When our second daughter was born, three years after we thought we were saying good-bye to Gampy, we had already decided to name her Poppy. As a boy and then a young man, Poppy was Gampy's nickname. I had never really heard people call him that, because he was Gampy to us, until one night when Henry and I watched a documentary about him.

One of the people being interviewed was an older gentleman named Bruce Gelb who had gone to boarding school with Gampy. He looked into the camera and recalled how he was picked on, teased, and bullied when he arrived at Andover. Then suddenly he heard the voice of an older boy rise up above the others and say, "Leave him alone!" And it was the voice of "Poppy" Bush. As the man told this story, decades later, he started wiping away tears, saying that because my grandfather had the goodness to stand up for him, his life was changed. (My grandfather has too much humility to tell us this story; I'm not surprised anymore when I learn something new about him by reading a book or watching an interview.)

I was newly pregnant, but far enough along that we knew it was a girl, and I looked over at Henry and said, "Maybe we should name the baby Poppy. That's the type of girl we want, somebody who will stand up for others and for what's right." So we did. When she was born, we FaceTimed Gampy from the hospital to introduce him to his great-granddaughter, named for him. And as soon as he saw her little pink face, he teared up, which I didn't expect because many people in our family, all of whom love him so much, have his name. Putting aside all the Georges—even among the girls there is a Georgia and Georgies—so we were by no means the first people to name our baby after him, although no one else has used his nickname. Once he started crying, we did too. Poppy's newborn head was covered in tears.

A couple of years ago in Maine, we were all sitting around the robin blue oval table that we've sat around for years having dinner—with Gampy at the head. The room was full of laughter. Everybody was talking, except for Gampy, and the conversation was ricocheting around the table. It started getting loud, and eventually he leaned over and in a hoarse voice, he whispered, "I miss this."

And I asked, "What, Gampy, what do you miss?"

And he looked around and said, "I loved being in the game. Don't forget to enjoy being part of the game."

Jenna and Gampy on the morning of his ninetieth birthday, before his big skydive.

A New Season

JENNA

It was mid-April in New York, cool but with canopies of new leaves and flowering trees, signs that winter had finally departed for good. On days like this, Manhattanites are overeager to move on to the next season: They sit wrapped in parkas at sidewalk cafés or run alongside the Hudson River tightly zipped into fleece.

I felt a bit of that same spring fever as I climbed out of bed in a room with barely enough space for our king frame and two tiny nightstands. But at eight months pregnant, I needed the strength of both arms to hoist myself up and over the side of the mattress. I was continually surprised by my size. I had reverse body dysmorphia; I couldn't tell how massive I had become except for the enormous effort that it took to do simple tasks.

In a cycling class that morning, a man who sat in front of me commented as I shimmied between the handle bars to get to my bike: "Girl, you are having that baby today...be careful or we will have to carry you out like a Trojan horse." I laughed. "The baby isn't coming for a few more weeks," I assured him.

Afterward, I squeezed into a bright-marigold-yellow dress, which, because of my protruding stomach, was short. Too short, really, for a grown pregnant woman. (During my next pregnancy, I wore that same dress on the *Today Show* and someone tweeted that I looked like Big Bird.) But I was tired of dark winter colors and thick, insulated tights. I was going to wear the yellow dress. I didn't even ask Henry for his opinion before we left the apartment. But on the sidewalk, I stood behind him, slightly embarrassed and afraid what might be revealed in the sunlight. As I hailed a cab, I kept tugging at the hem, wishing the dress would miraculously stretch and become a few inches longer. I was on my way to my baby shower, planned with meticulous detail by Barbara and many of my dearest friends.

I arrived to a room decorated with baby bottles filled with tiny blue and pink M&M's and cookies in the shapes of rattles. I usually love a good party, but as I entered, I didn't want to be there. I felt uncomfortable and anxious and kept fiddling with my dress. I avoided the center of the room, preferring to cluster in a corner of the apartment. When Barbara walked over, I grabbed her arm. "Stay here with me," I told her. "I can't talk to anyone else."

Barbara laughed. She reminded me that I was among friends. "Come on," she added, propelling me forward.

I still lagged behind. I felt an almost primal urge to hide, and I clung to the one who knew me from before I was born.

The caterer came by, but nothing looked appealing. I turned down a favorite food, a donut. When we got to the gift opening, the hostess clapped her hands and gathered us all together into a semicircle. I was ushered to the seat of honor in the center of the group, my temporary throne a lovely pink chair.

I opened pastel-paper-wrapped boxes filled with baby onesies and bottle warmers. I looked at the packaging, wondering, *How does a bottle warmer even work? Why does the baby even need warm milk?* Then came the bigger questions: *What type of mother will I be? Can I do this? Can I really protect this little person?*

The pile of discarded wrapping paper grew and we began to play a game: Each gift-giver made a prediction about the baby's gender (we had decided to be surprised) and the name.

"Boy! Harold Hager!" came one guess. I opened a set of yellow and white burp cloths.

"Boy! Rodrigo Hager," another friend chimed in.

I felt a shift in my stomach…it hurt. My friends sitting across from me on a matching pink-patterned couch laughed; the tight yellow dress showed everything. They could see what I felt.

"What was that?" someone asked. "Jenna, your water may break right here!"

I gave a halfhearted laugh and then tried to discreetly wipe a few small beads of sweat from my upper lip and pull down my hem again, before I opened a long rectangular box. Inside was a tiny turquoise-and-white polka-dot guitar. I loved it; I imagined a toddler strumming chords, singing nursery rhymes, creating songs, his or her voice a new sound track for our lives.

"I love that miniature guitar!" My sister said exactly what I thought, and not for the first time. "Pass it to me!"

Barbara tried to find the chords to the only song she remembered how to play, a Stone Temple Pilots piece she learned in seventh grade when she took guitar lessons twice a week. This was during the phase when she pierced her own belly button while listening to Led Zeppelin's "Tangerine" on repeat.

"Here it is...C...D," she said, laughing as the tiny guitar sounded the chords we had last heard in middle school. And I started to laugh, to really laugh.

Right when Barbara was getting to the chorus, I felt it: Out of my short dress came an explosion of water, like a tidal wave. It poured out through the dress, onto the chair, and all over the floor. The doctors had told me that my baby was breech—her head was up near my heart, which meant there was nothing to hold back the water except for her two tiny feet. So this definitely wasn't your typical water-breaking-at-a-baby-shower moment.

The next few minutes were an out-of-body experience, the way at moments of maximum panic your life might take on the quality of an old film, where you feel as if you are watching it all unfurl frame by frame. I watched my friends' mouths open in total shock; some burst into laughter, some screamed, jumping up and backing away as if in fear of being poisoned by my embryonic fluid. Another pregnant woman stared at me, horrified. Then tears started streaming down her face and she bolted into the powder room to avoid watching. The only male present—the caterer—threw a paper towel roll at me and abruptly walked out of the apartment, trays of artfully arranged hors d'oeuvres left behind, never to be eaten.

I started to laugh hysterically and then I cried.

"What do I do now?" I said, to everyone and no one.

Part of the joyful, nervous tears were because I had never fully believed that I would make it to this moment. The women in my mom's family are strong, but all the way back to my great-grandmother, the one thing that has proven very difficult for them was having children. Both my mother and my grandmother are only children, but not by choice. My great-grandmother, who could mix her own mortar and lay her own brick, buried at least two babies in the hot El Paso, Texas, ground, both of whom were "born too soon." My grandmother laid three children to rest after my mom, two boys and another little girl. One, named John Edward Welch, struggled for two days in Midland, Texas's primitive Western Clinic, wrapped in blankets and fed with an eyedropper.

My mom's earliest memory as a toddler is of being held up to the thick observation glass in her father's strong arms so she could see her brother, swaddled between life and death. After his two days on earth, he was called a "late miscarriage" and buried in a tiny coffin in an unmarked grave. Newnie Ellis, Midland's undertaker, placed him in the part of the cemetery reserved for the babies who had come ever so briefly into the world. A girl, Sarah Elizabeth, would join him some five years later, and then another premature boy whom they must have found too difficult to name.

My own mom had wanted a houseful of children, but it was not to be.

She and my dad struggled to get pregnant. They had put their names in with an adoption agency and were finally approved as candidates on the day that my mom found out she was expecting Barbara and me. At barely seven months along she almost lost us to preeclampsia, a condition of dangerously high blood pressure during pregnancy, which can lead to kidney failure and even death for the mother. She was flown out of Midland and put on bed rest for three weeks at Baylor Hospital in Dallas before we were born by Cesarean section. As we grew, she kept our cribs and baby furniture for years, still hoping. "My heart," she wrote, "was deep enough for more."

Growing up, Barbara and I always knew how very much we were wanted, that we had been the answer to our parents' prayers.

This baby wasn't my first baby either. There had been another one before. Henry and I hadn't even really been trying. I was working a lot. I had flown out to California to interview the actor Jake Gyllenhaal and I felt sick. Really sick. I called Henry at 4 a.m. and he told me to take a pregnancy test. So I did. I walked down to a drugstore near the hotel. I was nervous even going into the store to buy a pregnancy test; I didn't want anyone to recognize me and see what I was buying. I tried to camouflage it amid a water bottle, a pack of gum, and a tube of mascara. Back in the hotel bathroom, I laid the stick out on the counter and waited; the mark was positive. I was thrilled; it felt unbelievable because I knew how hard it had been for the women who came before me. I did the math and realized that I was almost eight weeks—two months—along.

I flew back to New York feeling as if I had a powerful secret inside me. Yet I was nervous, overwhelmingly nervous, with a sudden sense that this was too good to be true. I called my doctor. She was out of town, but she offered to drive in. I felt badly and said, "Well, no, don't do that. It's just that I've never done this before. I don't know anything. I don't know what I'm supposed to eat or what I'm supposed to do."

Still, I just couldn't shake the feeling that something was wrong. She must have heard my hesitation because she said that she needed to come in to run an errand and could easily stop by her office to do an ultrasound. I felt a small wave of relief. I thanked her, adding that I was traveling a lot for work, and "it would really be great to see the baby."

Henry was out of town in Norfolk, Virginia, so I went to the appointment by myself. I had told him that he didn't need to be there because it was just the first sonogram. I hadn't told anyone else, except a good friend from work, and even then, all I revealed was the very noncommittal "I might be pregnant."

I took a cab to the doctor's office. They did some blood work, and then I went into the exam room. The doctor, a lovely woman with a friendly face, walked in. She's Indian American, and in a comforting bit of symmetry, it was a female Indian American doctor who did the first sonogram of Barbara and me. The doctor smiled; she said that according to the blood test, "You're pregnant."

I thought, *Oh, thank goodness*. I was so relieved. She put some cool gel on my stomach and began running the ultrasound probe over my abdomen, where the baby was supposed to be. But there was nothing there. She kept circling the probe, and she asked, "You haven't had any fertility drugs, have you?" And I said no.

She said okay, but it was one of those slightly clipped "okays" that really mean nothing is okay. Slowly, she slid the probe in another direction. That's when she found the baby, growing inside my fallopian tube. It was, she informed me, an ectopic pregnancy. I didn't know what the words meant. She explained that the baby was growing not in my uterus, but in the fallopian tube, which delivers the egg. And because it was so far along, I had to go straight into emergency surgery. The tube could rupture at any moment, causing life-threatening internal bleeding. "You have an angel on your shoulder," she said to me.

It was crushing. I called Henry and told him to rush to the airport and back home. The next thing I knew, I was lying on a gurney with an IV in my arm being wheeled into surgery and feeling totally alone.

After I got home, I was still having a bad reaction to the anesthesia and felt horrible. I was up all night. And I cried. I cried for this loss. I lay in that bed thinking about my grandmother and my great-grandmother. I thought, *How could they have done this? How could they have survived this time after time?*

Barbara grabbed my hand. "It will be okay," she said calmly. She had no idea whether it would be or not; neither one of us had ever given birth, but I saw the steadiness in her eyes and I believed her. She and an older cousin and another friend who both already had children and had been through this several times sprang into action.

"*Call the Uber!*"

"*Call HENRY! Ask him to grab the overnight bag. NOW!*"

"*Someone pack up the donuts! They might get hungry at the hospital.*"

Barbara led me to the shower, away from the laughter and chaos of the living room, still adorned with bouquets of light-colored balloons.

While I was showering, Barbara called Henry. He was at a local rooftop restaurant, celebrating over beers with the boyfriends and husbands of the women at the shower. As Barbara spoke, all he heard in the background were the sounds of women talking and their laughter.

"Henry!" Barbara exclaimed. "We have to get to the hospital. Now. Jenna's water broke. It's time. Go home now, and throw some things into a bag: toothbrush—"

"Oh come on!" he said back. "We were at the doctor yesterday. She said it would be weeks. This isn't funny. You and Jenna have to stop with the practical jokes. This one isn't funny." And he hung up.

Years of April Fool's pranks, one of my favorite days of the year, and playing endless jokes on our parents and friends, as well as on the most unsuspecting of our subjects, Henry, came floating back, biting us in the ass.

"Henry doesn't believe us," Barbara told me as I stepped into the borrowed sweatpants and sweatshirt that belonged to my friend's husband and lined my pants with a towel.

"What are we going to do?" I asked. "Call him again."

The call went to voice mail. Henry wasn't answering.

Leaving the apartment was like leaving the scene of a crime. Many of the guests had already departed. Those who had stayed were picking up shreds of wrapping paper and placing them into a giant trash bag; someone else was mopping. The pink chair that I had been sitting in had already mercifully disappeared.

As I got into the Uber headed to the hospital to give birth—something that I still think of as a unique, New York City thing—I felt so far from home. Where was my mother? Where was my husband? My mind was racing with scenarios, until I looked over and saw Barbara, calmly riding with me, a box of donuts balanced on her lap.

After a friend of mine called her husband in a panic to tell him the mess that she had just witnessed, Henry finally rushed home to grab a bag. Barbara and I were capable of a lot of mischievous pranks, but he had realized that if someone else was claiming that my water broke, she must be telling the truth.

Henry arrived in the delivery room, and an hour later our darling daughter Margaret Laura (who we would come to call Mila), named after both of our mothers just as Barbara and I were, was born.

I still feel like the circle of women who just hours earlier had been so sure that Mila was a boy made her decide to stand up and announce herself: "Wait, world, here I come, and I am *not* a boy! I am woman; hear me roar!"

———————

The first person to meet Mila, minus Henry and me of course, was Barbara. She held her so naturally, seemingly not worried about her fragile six-pound body. When it was time to take a picture of our new family of three, Barbara was appalled by the hospital's fluorescent lighting and the shadows it created on my already exhausted face, so she wheeled my hospital bed to the window, where the sun was shining.

"Let's use some of that natural light," she said. Henry thought we were insane. The nurses and doctors walking in must have thought the same.

But that first picture of me holding my baby, taken by my sister, the person who was born alongside me, was perfect and perfectly warmed by the light of a new season.

Continuing the sister photo tradition: Jenna and Henry's first photo with Poppy, taken by Barbara with sunlight and love on lucky August 13, 2015.

Sisters First and Last

BARBARA

At thirteen, waiting inside a strip mall in Austin for my orthodontist, Dr. Hooten, to tighten my braces, I discovered a *Vogue* magazine. It was like a secret treasure, a genie lamp smelling of traces of detachable perfume samples. Stephanie Seymour, in a famed Steven Meisel image, graced the cover in a power suit. I didn't know this type of glamour or sophistication existed. I quietly slipped the magazine into my bag and spirited it home after Dr. Hooten tightened my "clear" braces (which, um, never looked clear but were always slightly tinted brown). I read and reread that *Vogue* cover to cover. I carefully cut out the best photos, covering the walls of my tiny green-and-white bedroom with images of beautiful, exotic landscapes and '90s Calvin Klein ads of Kate Moss and Vincent Gallo. It was a stark contrast to my governor's mansion room, a onetime sleeping porch built to escape the baking-hot Austin summers, a room that the previous governor, Ann Richards, had used as a closet.

That *Vogue* was my catalyst: I decided that one day, I would leave Texas.

New York was my first stop. In eighth grade our small Episcopal middle school offered an optional trip to New York City over Thanksgiving. It was magic. Our crowd of girls wandered outside all day long—a concept that did not exist in hot, suburban Texas—walking to museums, exploring Chinatown and Central Park, and gazing at the Christmas windows that had sprung up along Fifth Avenue. The sun set around 4:30, but that didn't matter as the city—or at least in my memories of it—was brightly lit and sparkled at all hours. I listened to the rumble of buses and the honk of yellow cabs and the clicking of women's heels on the sidewalk. I was mesmerized by the clipped New York speech with its run-together words, rather than slow, drawn-out vowels, and the lilt of foreign accents. Almost everyone was clothed in black. The women wore their hair not big and full, but in careless, uneven shags or pin-straight, glossy, and slicked back. At age fourteen, I wanted to move to New York as soon as possible.

A decade later, I did in fact end up in New York, just as I had promised myself. A couple of years ago as I walked through the West Village, I passed a man on the sidewalk along Sixth Avenue. Arranged around him were used books and stacks of old magazines, with the Stephanie Seymour *Vogue* right on top. I stopped and flipped through the pages, remembering. He offered to give it to me, but I didn't buy or take it. The way my life has turned out is in some ways better than any adventure I could have imagined after reading that magazine years ago. While I did move away, my life did not. My sister followed me to the city. We now live four blocks apart. Just as I used to spend the night in her room, I can now spend the night in her apartment. My nieces pop over anytime to see Auntie Barbara. We are still intertwined in each other's lives.

As part of my work with Global Health Corps, we ask our fellows to share why they do this work, why they want to be in global health. I will never forget one Burundian fellow's answer. Alida grew up with several brothers and sisters; many of them were the children of friends that her parents had taken in during years of bloody civil war. They treated all the children equally, regardless of whether they were related. On birthdays in her family, rather than being showered with presents and treated as someone special, you were asked to make the case of why, in the previous year, you had lived the best year that you could. You did get a cake, but first you had to share what you had done for other people and how you had contributed.

I was struck by the profound idea, even for little kids: the concept that you needed to make a case that you were living life in a way that was worth it, in a way that was giving to others. You are here for a reason, and you should be grateful for every year, and be ready to do the most with the next one.

For my entire time on this earth, I will share my birthday, and my life meaning, with one other person: my sister. There were three hearts inside my mama's body before we were born—her heart, my heart, and the heart I know so well: Jenna's.

JENNA

The world has often compared Barbara and me, but our parents never did. I realize now how easy it would have been to quip: Jenna, your sister, never acts that way! Your sister doesn't impulsively kick a soccer ball into our front window! Or why don't you make As like your sister? And because of that, the bond we shared from before birth was solidified. I was never jealous of Barbara (although I should have been envious of her near-perfect SAT score!) and she wasn't jealous of me. Her successes were my successes; her heartbreaks were also mine.

I did have a boyfriend who, while staring into my eyes, said, "I wish your eyes were like your sister's." I wanted to yell: "No shit! I love the color of her eyes!"

Recently, Melinda Gates (Barbara's ultimate girl crush) tweeted an article about Barbara. I was riding the subway and saw the tweet during a brief respite with Wi-Fi—and I wanted to yell out to all the passengers: *"See, my sister is a Global Health star! Even Melinda Gates knows that she's saving the world!"*

When people stop me and inquire about my more elusive sister, they typically ask, "Is she married?" I understand their curiosity, but internally I beg them to ask about what she's doing. I want to tell them about the work she does, about the nonprofit she started all by herself, about all that she's accomplished.

And recently I did just that. A woman at an event asked in a worried tone: "Why isn't your sister married?" I took a deep breath and responded, "She is married. To her work, Global Health Corps. You can google it. Oh, and she has a nice boyfriend too."

Was it too extreme? Maybe. But that is what sisters do— they want what is best for each other. They always protect each other.

Not too long ago, I picked Mila up from her preschool. She

smiled her wide smile and said, "Mama!" (a word I will never tire of hearing).

"Where is Poppy? I want Poppy-Lou," she sang.

I picked her up and held her, inhaling her silky hair, smelling school on her: paste, paint, and oranges. It made me long for my sister, the way she longed for hers.

I remembered walking into new schools, meeting new kids: together. Walking into spaces where we felt out of place: hands entwined.

As I walked Mila home, I thought of my sister, now all grown up. She was in Africa. What was she doing? Preparing for bed? Was she staring into the Rwandan sky, looking at other stars that created different patterns from the ones we would soon see muted by the brilliant lights of Manhattan?

That night, I held my girls closely and listened to the patterns of their breathing until they were in sync, until they were one.

You have each other, I thought to myself. *You can walk through this wild and wonderful life together. You will fight, yes. And you will adapt to each other's quirks, but you will do it together. You will make your sister feel like she is enough. And for me, your mama, well, that is enough. More than enough. That is everything.*

Acknowledgments

Sisters First isn't a typical memoir, but rather a love story we wrote to each other. We always dreamed of writing a book, but the timing never seemed right. When we woke up together (Henry was out of town) on November 9, 2016, we were filled with gratitude that we had each other for comfort. Then we realized it didn't start with just that moment. We had each other's back through all the moments that had come before. First days of school, first heartbreaks, first jobs, campaigns, elections—we could always rely on one another for support and encouragement. That deep connection, that amazing sense of sisterhood felt so empowering and, on that day after Election Day, when the world felt so divided, we couldn't help but think about how awesome it would be if other women throughout our country and throughout the world could recognize their sisters and the sister-like people in their lives who gave them strength. Our bookish mom always advocated the power of storytelling, so we thought we'd start there, sharing our own stories in the hope they will inspire readers to celebrate the power of sisterhood. That's the kind of world we want Mila and Poppy to grow up in.

And so we are grateful to Lyric Winik, who gave us the confidence to write about some of our most personal memories, and to the outstanding team at Hachette: Suzanne O'Neill (who we like to call SUZZAAANNEE), Nidhi Pugalia, Andrew Duncan, Jimmy Franco, Amanda Pritzker, Anne Twomey, Carolyn Kurek, Thomas Louie, Karen Kosztolnyik, Ben Sevier, Michael Pietsch, and all those who helped us along the way.

And also great appreciation to the crew at CAA: Cait Hoyt and Kate Childs, you epitomize strong sisterhood and could take over the world if you wanted. Thanks to Christina Piasta, Caroline Floeck, and Mary Finch. Thanks to Darnell, Rachel, and Olivia for supporting this idea from the beginning. We will never forget that first meeting.

Thanks to all the early readers: Henry, Sarah B, Caroline, Elise, Mike, Savannah, Mera, Lauren, Jinxy, Stephen, Dorothy, Mama, and Popsicle. Those days spent editing the first draft meant so much.

Henry, thanks for loving our sisterhood enough to give us this time together and for being one of the sweetest parts of our stories. We both love you (one of us a little more!).

And of course the most sincere appreciation to our parents and grandparents. You taught us what it means to love, how to love each other, and always allowed us to be ourselves.

238

About the Authors

Jenna Bush Hager is a correspondent on NBC's *Today Show* and an editor-at-large for *Southern Living* magazine. She is the author of the *New York Times* bestseller *Ana's Story: A Journey of Hope*, written after she served as an intern with UNICEF in Latin America. She also co-authored the children's books *Our Great Big Backyard* and *Read All About It!* with her mother. She lives with her husband and two daughters in New York.

Barbara Pierce Bush is the CEO and co-founder of Global Health Corps, an organization that mobilizes a global community of young leaders to build the movement for health equity. GHC has mobilized almost one thousand young leaders who believe health is a human right and who take an innovative approach to solving some of the world's biggest global health challenges. Previously, Barbara worked at the Smithsonian's Cooper-Hewitt, National Design Museum and Red Cross Children's Hospital in South Africa, and interned with UNICEF in Botswana.